ANATOMY OF ERRORS

"Idleness is the parent of all psychology"

Nietzshe

ANATOMY
OF ERRORS

The good (and not-so-good) reasons
we have for making the same old
mistakes over and over again

Alex Howard

Gateway Books, Bath

First published in 1989
by Gateway Books
The Hollies, Wellow,
Bath, BA2 8QJ

Cover design by Studio B, Bristol
Set in 10 on 12pt Andover
by Photosetting and Secretarial Services of Yeovil
Printed and bound by Billings of Worcester

British Library Cataloguing in Publication Data:
Howard, Alex
   Anatomy of errors: a self-help
   course in problem solving.
   1. Personality. Self-evaluation – Questions
   & answers
   I. Title
   155.2'5'076
            ISBN 0-946551-44-8

Foreword

There are still many errors in this book; many details that I am less than happy with and would like to change. It is not, I hope, the 'best' that I can do!

In these respects it illustrates what I am seeking to show; which is that you, and I, need to come to terms with some of the ways in which we are (all) – let's face it – *mediocre!*

Many best sellers promise (pretend) to show how you can be a Super-Executive, Superwoman, Super Salesman, Supermum, Super-Successful... whatever. Here, I am going to argue that real success derives from coming to terms with, and making good use of, the ordinary, mediocre and everyday-averageness of ourselves and others. In this way, rather than through our dreams of being 'super', we can get more fun out of life, and make better use of our options, strengths and limitations.

To Jane:
My fellow 'expert in error'
– with love.

Preface

We all like to think that we are 'sensitive' and 'sensible'; and yet my behaviour (and *yours!*) often appears to me to be absurd, irrational, self-defeating and destructive.

We all like to believe that we learn from our mistakes and that, although we grow older, at least we get a little wiser. Yet sometimes it seems that we never learn and that we go on making the same mistakes over and over again.

Why do we go on making crazy mistakes and why does our behaviour often seem to us to be perfectly sensible at the time, yet disastrous when we later pause to consider what we did? Do we always have genuinely good reasons for doing what we do, and if we *are* to change, do we need to find out what these reasons are?

Our behaviour may seem sensible, right, reasonable and proper to us when we are in the midst of action; yet what looks best in the heat of the moment may often turn out to be 'second best' or 'tenth best'. Why is this?

In the following pages I will try to grapple with these questions and, hopefully, provide a few helpful hints. (Though no 'final answers' – needless to say!) As the title suggests, I will be attempting an *Anatomy of Errors*; an examination of our biggest and commonest mistakes, and the ('good' and 'sensible') reasons why we make them.

I hope that, as a result, you will get a clearer and deeper picture of some of your options, motives, and conflicts. What you do with this (hopefully) deeper understanding is of course, and rightly, entirely up to you!

Introduction

Do you sometimes make the same old mistakes with the same problems over and over again? Do you ever get into the same old familiar mess even when faced with new and very different problems? If you're anything like me you will have answered 'yes' on both counts!

We can, of course, make a unique and individual 'mess' of individual and particular problems. Less obviously, perhaps, we each have a repertoire of key – 'all-purpose' – errors that we make in a wide variety of situations; with a large range of problems! There are, I suggest, certain kinds of mistake that people repeatedly make regardless of the problem they are dealing with. We seem to have a 'Top Ten' *Hit List* of errors that we make day after day. It is this kind of error that I want to explore in these pages.

You may think that emotional problems are very different from practical/technical problems, and that these in turn are quite different from social or intellectual or other personal difficulties that we face. In some ways, of course, they *are* all different. But have you ever stopped to consider the *similarities*?

For example, consider the kind of mess that you can sometimes get into with your partner; and compare this with the difficulties that sometimes overwhelm you when you are on your own at the workplace or kitchen table. On the surface of things these problems may not seem to resemble each other at all. They may look and feel quite different. But even if the effects may be very different the causes of these problems may be very similar. It may well be that, insofar as you've made any mistakes in the way you tackled them, you made the same errors with your spouse as you did in other, quite different, situations. You may doubt this. If so, please read on and let me try to persuade you.

Perhaps you are making a piece of furniture, seeking a major contract, trying to pass an exam, thinking about a divorce, planning your retirement, recovering from a bereavement, sewing on a button, getting the children to school, looking for a job. In every case we can make specific errors arising from our ignorance of the particular problem; or we can make the more lethal sort of mistake which is the result of our erroneous approach to problem-solving in general.

When we lack specific expertise or information about a problem we, in effect, don't know enough about its *content*; and so the consequent errors that we make can be crudely described as 'Content Errors'. Sometimes, though, what is wrong is our whole *process*, or method, of approaching problems; let's call these 'Process Errors'.

I don't want to suggest that the distinction between Process and Content is a hard and fast one that works on every occasion. But it will do for now. It will not serve as a means of providing new theory about human behaviour. But it will, I think, provide some practical tips about dealing with problems. You will, I hope, get a much better picture of what I mean by a 'process error' when you come to look at the examples of this kind of mistake in the following chapter.

This book will tell you nothing about the specific, individual errors you can make with specific, individual problems. Every instruction manual, or textbook (on whatever subject), that ever existed will tell you something about these. However, I have come across very few beginners' books that look systematically at 'process-errors', and this simple introduction is a limited attempt to fill that gap.

The *content* of our problems obviously varies a very great deal, but, if you think about it, you may find that you quite often go through the same *process* of making a mess of your problems regardless of their content. If you haven't thought about this before, let me invite you to do so in the next few hundred pages! I don't, though, want to give the impression that this is going to be a book about 'Brain Teasers' and 'Logic-Chopping'.

There is a tendency to believe that problem-solving is an entirely mental, intellectual, logical matter involving no more than rational enquiry and the examination of ideas and the logical relationships between them. I hope it will become increasingly clear, as we go along, that the subject needs to be seen far more broadly than that. A person who tries to approach problems of any kind and who ignores his (and other people's) feelings, motives, intentions, values and internal conflicts is going to make a very poor job of many of his or her problems.

Effective problem-solving, in other words, is not a cold, arid, detached enquiry after 'Truth'. It frequently involves passion and commitment of every sort; our own and other people's; in mild and subtle forms as well as strong and dramatic varieties. We ignore this at our peril.

Consequently, you will find that, although some time is given over to more obviously 'intellectual' mistakes of thinking and reasoning, even more space is allotted in this book to errors that are a result of emotional and moral 'inadequacies' or 'immaturity'. And this, I hope to show, is quite appropriate.

We are obsessed, these days, with technical/technological solutions to all difficulties; and consequently we are too entranced by machinery and we live too much in our heads. Much of the personal and collective mess that we make with our lives, does not, in fact, arise from logical and technological inadequacies at all. It is a result of moral failure and emotional immaturity. This may sound like a rather old fashioned remark to make, and I'm certainly not advocating a return to Puritanism. But it needs to be said all the same.

We keep on looking for new techniques to get us out of difficulties that have arisen not from any technical failure but from amoral, or emotionally repressive or indulgent behaviour. On other occasions, we run into difficulties not so much because we have been irrational or immoral, but because we have taken an overly narrow and restricted view of what constitutes rational behaviour.

However, let me make it clear, I am not intending to take an anti-rational, anti-intellectual approach to problem-solving. On the contrary. Thoughts and feelings are inexorably intertwined; and the trouble, so often, is that people who set so much store by the power of their minds are in fact very often dominated by emotions they won't face. And, at the other extreme, those who set so much store by their feelings are in fact governed by a restricted number of (unexamined, unexplored and therefore generally simplistic) ideas and beliefs! More of this later.

In the next section you will find a questionnaire which lists sixty-nine key errors that we can make regardless of the problem we face. You are invited to read through this and pick out those pitfalls that seem to apply most often to you. Some of these will be familiar to you. Others, you will recognise at once even though you have never considered or been aware of them before.

I have tried to design this book so that you can either read it in the normal way, from cover to cover, or follow up on those sections that seem to be particularly relevant to you. The book tries to make the subject as simple and as readable as possible. But a lot of material is presented in quite a short amount of space, it interlinks in complex ways; and so it may be best to avoid trying to read too much at any one time! In some ways the book is like a practical manual, except that it does not offer neat and easy answers. (There aren't any!)

Every book has its limits; so let me make a few defensive and apologetic remarks.

Firstly, it *is* just a book; just words on pages; and so it can never be a substitute for real personal human contact. This is relevant because you will make a lot more progress with 'problem solving/coping/surviving' if you can share problems with others – with integrity and real mutual respect. In other words, although this is a practical 'Self-Help' book it does not advocate that you should try to do everything on your own!

Secondly: everything that is said here could be usefully explored in much more detail. But there is a limit to what can be done in a few hundred pages. What follows takes a very broad sweep and so inevitably it does less than full justice to many topics.

Thirdly, the questionnaire method depends on your being able to recognise the particular process errors you are making. There is plenty of evidence to show that people can recognise, from a checklist of possibilities, far more than they can recall with their own unaided efforts. But there are limits to this.

There may well be some key errors you are making that you will not recognise, even though they are listed in the following questionnaire. This may be because you are not ready to recognise them (in which case fair enough), or because you need more immediate human support and personal contact in order to be able to see what is going on. In other words, here is another important limitation of any practical book on self-help psychology.

I have explored sixty-nine ways in which you can 'make a mess' of virtually any sort of problem. I have also made some practical suggestions about what you can do about it; and, in many cases, the remedy is clear as soon as you have discovered the mistake! Inevitably, though, there is much more that could be said about practical remedies.

However, let me suggest the following to those of you who start to say "But *how* can I change? What can I do? Give me more clues, more practical hints, more details." Ask yourself: "Is it *really* the case that I don't know how to get out of this mess?" It may sometimes be that you *do* know and that you also know why you are not taking action.

For example, suppose you discover that procrastination is one of your weaknesses. You tend to keep putting things off; delaying and avoiding action. You then say "What can I do?" Well, isn't the answer obvious? The question is quite likely to be just another cop-out! It's just another delaying tactic!

Sometimes, people say "O.K. so I know that I need to 'jump in'; but how do I jump?" The answer? They already know how to jump, and asking 'how' is just another avoidance tactic. The question is, *will* they?

There is an even more useful question that is worth considering: rather than asking "How do I jump?" try asking "How do I *avoid* jumping? How do I stay on the side?" There are many possible answers to this one, and a large number of these will be examined in the following pages.

Finally, this book is based on the assumption that we can become more self-aware and that, as a result of this awareness, we can make changes in the way we behave. In this respect I am an optimist. However, my optimism is guarded and cautious. I am sure that there are substantial limits on the extent to which we can change our behaviour or become conscious of what we think and do. We can throw some light on ourselves and our behaviour; but, like a candle, this light reveals that the **dark mysterious shadows of our helplessness and ignorance are much larger than the bright centres of our power and knowledge!** As we discover more about how and why we think, feel and behave as we do, we become ever more aware of just how much we *don't know*. Most of our behaviour and thought remains an enigma to us. This is a book for beginners, yet, to be honest, on the subject of psychology we are essentially all beginners. We remain our own greatest mystery.

Questionnaire: "The problems that I have with this problem"

You may find it useful to categorise your responses to the statements listed below as follows:

!!	very much applies to me
!	applies to me to some extent
x	this does not apply to me
?	I don't know whether or not this applies to me
??	I don't understand this statement

Problems arising from a lack of COURAGE:

Problems arising from a lack of COURAGE, LOVE and WISDOM:

Problems arising from a lack of COURAGE:

1. I need to **face up** to my problem rather than run away from it.

It is very easy, when we face up to a problem, to find ourselves getting tense, as though we were expecting to be attacked by our 'adversary'. This probably goes back to the days when our problems really did have teeth and claws! Nowadays, mostly, they won't actually strike at us; and they certainly won't do so when we are merely *thinking* about problems and trying to sort them out in our minds. So, see if you can relax. There is no need to tense up and grit your teeth at the thought of dealing with a problem. It won't hit you; and reminding yourself of this may actually help you to relax!

You think you would be better off if you faced up to this problem? No doubt there are also times when you want to run away from it! You will probably feel in conflict with yourself about it sometimes.

What happens when you tell yourself "I need to face this problem"? What sort of attitude do you take to yourself? Is your 'voice of conscience' a harsh and domineering *tyrant* or is it like a firm and supportive friend? You won't deal with problems very well if you are too hard on yourself.

Are you the sort of person who is too severe, intolerant and unforgiving with yourself? If so, then do you notice that, after you have 'beaten yourself up' about how bad you are, you often go to the other extreme and say "to hell with it all. I can't face it, I won't face it, I'm terribly tired, weak, hopeless" etc.

A firm and gentle approach will help to stop you swinging wildly between the two extremes of saying "I must, I must...!" and "I can't, I won't...!" You may say, "I must, must, must... tackle this problem", and maybe a part of you actually *wants* to deal with it. Frequently, when people say they 'must' do something, they actually mean they want to because of either external or internal 'pressures'. Conversely, when you say "I *can't* deal with it" are you sure that you don't actually mean you *won't*? "I must, but I can't face this problem!" often means "I want to, *and* I don't want to". That is to say, we are in conflict with ourselves about it. (And this kind of internal conflict is very common!)

Facing up to the problem may well be in your own, and other people's best interest in the long run. But have you noticed that, in the short run, it may often be uncomfortable to tackle that task? What is best for us in the longer term quite often conflicts with what seems most comfortable in the short run; and, to make it worse, we tend to live and think with only short term horizons in mind. This, as we shall see, is the source of many of our difficulties!

So what is to be done? Avoiding a problem generally gets us nowhere, yet facing it can be painful. If you mistakenly try to make your life free of all pain, you can go after short term comfort, get stuck, and end up worse off in the longer term. How many times have you suffered as a result of this? How many of your friends are in difficulties as a result of this classic error?

We don't *have* to stay stuck, though. One useful, first, commonsense, step is to build up a clear picture (or sensation or message) in your mind of the benefits that you will have as a result of dealing with this problem. See if you can make this picture as vivid, bright and as detailed as you can.

Now compare this idea with the inferior alternative: of what life will be like for you if you carry on doing nothing about this problem. This, too, will be more effective the more you can get a really graphic, (but dark, grey, gloomy) picture of the price you will have to pay!

Two thoughts then: One, of what it will be like if you tackle the problem; the other, of what will probably happen if you don't! If you hold these two images next to each other in your mind you will often discover plenty of incentives to get on with the job, despite the short run discomfort and difficulty.

You may think, "That's fairly obvious. There is nothing very deep or profound about that." And, indeed, there isn't! Furthermore there is nothing very new about this approach. It is precisely the method that we all generally use when we do decide to take action with a problem.

Quite simply, the way to take action is to pay closer attention to the *benefits* of action and the *costs* of inaction. And, conversely, if you want to stay stuck and inactive you simply do the opposite. You endlessly preoccupy yourself with thoughts of how painful and uncomfortable it might be if you try to do anything and you compare this with the (short-term) comfort of inaction. That way you can stay stuck indefinitely. And this is precisely the way people *do* stay stuck!

So, if you want to stay inert, set your mind thinking about how something *can't* be done and how it would be too difficult, risky and uncomfortable. Sure enough, you will stay where you are. And if you want to move on, start thinking about how something *can* and *should* and *will* be done, and think about the benefits. You don't ignore the difficulties, of course. But instead of thinking about how these can defeat you, you instead set your mind to sorting out how you can overcome the problems.

The 14th Dalai Lama made the same point when he said:

"... if you want to know what will happen to you in the future, look at what your mind is doing now." (For the record, he also said: *"If you want to know what you were doing in the past, look at your body now"!)*

2. I could handle this problem more effectively if I was more tolerant of inevitable **confusion**.

Do you feel confused because you know too little about the problem? ... or because you know 'too much'! Maybe you have discovered new information which doesn't fit in easily with what you already knew. Confusion can be a sign that you are badly organised; (in which case see sections 26, 27, 29, 30, 62 and 65). But it can also arise because you are 'on the move' and are beginning to make some progress.

Do you never feel confused? Maybe you are a highly organised person. Or are you 'clear' because you are somewhat too rigid

and prejudiced? Are you ever prepared to let go of what you
know now and try to come to grips with something new? Some
people avoid feeling confused by avoiding anything new, or by
making everything fit in with what they already know. They stay
prejudiced and stuck and after a while they start to complain that
there is not enough in life that is new and challenging. Life seems
dull and predictable; "the same old things; nothing new under the
sun; I've seen it all before."

If you think you already know; or that there is nothing new
worth knowing, then you will avoid confusion. Instead you will
feel bored, jaded and stuck. We all hang on to ideas and methods
that have worked well enough for us in the past and, up to a
point, this makes sense. But there is plenty that is new and
surprising and different going on around you and within you all
the time. Are you prepared to look? Are you willing to be
confused? Are you willing to let go of old and familiar ways of
seeing things? Are you willing to go through the confusion that
arises when we move on from using one set of ideas to new ways
of thinking, seeing and behaving?

3. I **pretend** that I am more confused than I am in order to avoid facing up to the problem.

When you face up to (a part of) 'the truth' about yourself, other
people or your circumstances it can sometimes be very painful,
can't it? You may find confusion uncomfortable on occasions, but
have you noticed that there are times when *clarity* is even more
painful than confusion? When this happens, the pretence of
'confusion' can be like a safe haven from cold, hard reality!

Have you sometimes suspected that you know far more about
a problem than you realise? Do you make full use of what you
already know? And do you trust yourself sufficiently and give
yourself the credit you deserve?

You may be *pretending* to yourself that you are more confused than you really are because:
... You are scared of taking responsibility for the problem
... You are scared of facing up to your feelings about the problem
... You have a low opinion of yourself and of your ability to deal with the problem.
Pretending that you are confused can then become an escape *from all these uncomfortable realities.*

In the short run, such a pretence of 'confusion' is the easy way out; but in the longer run it means that you are running away from your life and failing to get to grips with your problem. There may well be a price that, sooner or later, you will have to pay.

4. I need to take a few **risks** and make a few **mistakes**.

Obviously, we all prefer to avoid mistakes if we can; and some mistakes, of course *are* avoidable with proper care. A careless, thoughtless and reckless approach clearly leads to errors that you would have been wiser to avoid. If you are too careless, you probably won't learn from your mistakes and you will be likely to cause needless pain and suffering to yourself and others.

But perhaps you are at the other extreme. Are you the sort of person who tries so hard to avoid making mistakes that you paralyse yourself? Are you stiff and clumsy in your actions because you are trying so hard to be careful and to stay in control? Do you watch what you are doing so much that this distracts you from actually *doing* it? If so, you won't learn very much because, more often than not, we have to learn by doing, and learn from our mistakes.

Are you the sort of person who won't do anything until you can be sure that you will do it right? If so, have you noticed that you are stuck in a 'Catch 22' situation? You want to do something very well; but you'll never learn to do it well unless you are prepared to begin by doing it badly!

See if you can be relaxed about tackling the problem badly, and really learn from this. You will then be far more likely to learn to do it well. The greatest mistake of all is to refuse to make any mistakes. One of the riskiest things you can do, is to refuse to take any risks! Because there is then an (extremely high) risk that you will feel stale, bored, stuck, unfulfilled and dissatisfied with yourself.

One of the greatest obstacles to learning anything – perhaps *the* greatest obstacle – is the fear of making a mistake. So often, people fail to learn something new, not because they lack the intelligence, but because they are too tense and insecure; too worried that they will 'get it wrong' and 'make fools of themselves', too concerned that they are not as good as they would like to be, or as good as other people are. And so it is that, when people compare themselves too much with what the 'high flyer' can achieve, they lose morale, lose enthusiasm, feel dejected about their skills and potential... and give up trying!

This leads to a terrible waste of potential and to the loss of all the joys involved in making full use of the skills we have. By definition, only a small minority of people can become the 'superstars' of their chosen field of interest. But does this mean that the rest of us should give up? Of course not! Thanks to television and the other media, we can now all see the very best of talent in entertainments, arts, sciences and every other field of interest. This provides a marvellous opportunity for us; but sadly it often seems to lead to people spending too much time as spectators of others and abandoning their own active interests on the grounds that... "there is no point, because I'm no good really; I could never be anywhere near as good as so-and-so that I read about or saw on television."

In schools nowadays this danger of paralysis and despair through comparing ourselves with the 'high-flyers' or the 'A-stream' class is perhaps more commonly recognised than it was in the past. But, in order to deal with it, another mistake is sometimes made. This is the error of attempting to camouflage the differences in ability and achievement that exist; and playing down and avoiding talk of differences. Such strategems, I think, can often be self-defeating. They assume that if children find out that they are not the smartest in a given subject then they are bound to become disillusioned, and so need to be protected by hiding or denying individual differences.

The very act of assuming that children will be discouraged by the 'terrible' news that they are not the brightest is itself discouraging for children. It actually encourages them to feel disillusioned! Because, of course, children (and adults) soon find out who is achieving the most in any given subject and are rightly curious to know how well they are doing compared with others. Surely the most useful approach is to be open about relative grades etc. but to encourage a child to avoid the (erroneous) idea that it is a 'catastrophe' if others can do something better than we can!

It is important to try to use our potential to the full, if only because to do so can be so personally satisfying. But it is even more important to realise that we do not have to be wonderful all the time, and that it is quite O.K., and overwhelmingly likely, that others will achieve more than we do. Moreover, it is only exceptionally that we will even manage to do *our own* best. After all, by definition, we are going to have to spend most of our time turning out no more than our average performance; and, for as often as we do exceptionally well, we must expect to do exceptionally badly in relation to our own average!

You will learn to be as good as you can be in everything, if you allow yourself to be, and to feel O.K. about being as bad as you presently are. See if you can trust yourself, relax, and have confidence in yourself. Don't wait until you have formed the 'perfect plan-of-action', because you will never get this. You won't even get a half-decent plan if you are not prepared to take some action! You don't stay in control by 'holding in' and 'holding on' all the time. This is a sign of a *lack* of control. Real competence and control comes from being prepared to let go and 'dive in' sometimes; even though there is uncertainty and risk involved.

You can find the right balance for you in all this, if you trust yourself.

5. I am hoping that the problem will **go away** all by itself.

Just sometimes (but not very often) a problem goes away all by itself if you leave it alone and do nothing about it. Problems don't very often go away 'all by themselves', (it's rather rare, in fact!) but they do so just often enough for us to be able to make use of this excuse!

Perhaps the present moment is really *not* the best time to deal with your problem. Perhaps you are not in the right mood; you do not have enough information; it is not a good moment for other people, etc.

On the other hand, are you avoiding the problem because it's the easiest way out? When we let short-term comfort triumph over longer-term well-being, we are, in fact, *running away* from our problems, and we often pay a very high price! Because we then have the problem 'hanging over us' for far longer than was necessary, with all the stress and tension that this involves. Furthermore, problems, generally speaking, get more difficult and urgent if we ignore them for too long. And so, what might have been relatively easy to deal with if tackled promptly, becomes a far more forbidding proposition the longer we leave it.

You can then find yourself in a vicious cycle: The more you put things off, the harder they are to face up to. And the harder they are to face, the more you put off facing them! If you get a clear picture in your mind of the long-term price you will have to pay, you will find that you can become much more motivated to get on with things without delay.

Of course, it is not always easy to decide what is best. Should you act now? Should you wait for a better moment? The answer is that there *is* no simple answer to this question. We just need to trust our own judgement about it. If you are prepared to be honest with yourself and get to the heart of the matter, you will *usually* know whether or not you are 'copping out', or running away from your problems. It is silly to complain that you don't know enough when you are not even making full use of what you *do* know!

6. I am reading this as a way of **avoiding** the problem.

Are you the sort of person who gathers more and more information about a problem, seemingly without end, without ever actually taking any action? Do you keep on 'discovering' new distractions that seem more interesting than the job in hand? What other tactics do you have for putting things off, and for pretending that *now* is not the best time to be facing the problem?

Even when you are well prepared and well organised, do you say to yourself "There is more than I need to know. It would be useful if I just sorted out my ideas a little more."? Do you go on trying to make a 'perfect plan' (as if there could ever be such a thing) and forgetting that it is ultimately the *action* that counts?

If so, then the remedy is obvious. Action! And if you say that you are "not absolutely sure; not entirely clear yet", then this may well be just one more delaying tactic!

7. I am trying to deal with this problem **prematurely**.

Mostly, people put things off for too long rather than rush into problems too quickly; but it does happen that we sometimes go at a problem before we are properly prepared and informed, and before the appropriate time to deal with it.

The commonest reason for this is that we don't like to feel the problem hanging over us, with all the uncertainty and insecurity that seems to be involved. Thus the mad dash to get the problem out of the way and 'off our backs'. "Any outcome," we start to think, "would be better than not knowing what the outcome will be."

Again, the remedy is obvious as soon as we become aware of

what we are doing. We need to be more patient, and more tolerant of (inevitable) uncertainty, doubt, internal conflict and insecurity; because there are times when all these feelings *are* inevitable.

There are times when you need to allow problems to hang, unresolved, 'in the air' sometimes, or else you will rush in prematurely and make many more mistakes than is necessary or desirable. And if you don't like to think of problems as 'hanging over' you, then create a new image of them that seems less threatening. For example, imagine them tucked away securely in some snug place where you can retrieve them whenever you want to! (But avoid *burying* them!)

It is just not realistic to expect that everything can always be tidy, neat and clear. And if you try to tidy everything up by rushing into things too quickly you will find that, ultimately, the problems are even less tidy, organised and sorted out than they would have otherwise been.

8. I am bothering myself with **someone else's** problem.

Do you like to take the role of 'rescuer' of other people? Do you enjoy taking responsibility for other people's problems? Do you like to give them your expert and excellent advice, and generally try to make decisions for them and 'save' them from themselves and their own folly?

This pattern of behaviour is commonly to be found with parents who are reluctant to recognise that their children are growing up and that they can, and should, be allowed to make decisions for themselves without too much interference from mum or dad. Also it sometimes happens that the husband or wife will try to act like a parent in relation to his or her spouse and take on the other person's problems as if they were their own. Indeed, there are plenty of people who quite like to play the role of helpless, passive child or 'victim' and who encourage others to take over the running of their lives.

In the long run, it does you no good to get other people to run your life for you; and you are running away from your own life if you spend too much time minding other people's business rather than looking after your own. This is a classic syndrome for many people involved in the 'helping' professions, and for managers who won't delegate!

People behave like this because you can feel quite good about yourself when you go around being the 'saviour' of others. And it often seems easier to find solutions to other people's problems than to your own, because you can see through their rationalisations far more easily than yours!

Hence, by bothering about other people's business, you can run away from your own (frightening) problems and pretend to yourself that you are doing this for the highest motives. Indeed, you can be so busy interfering in other people's lives that you can completely forget about and ignore what is happening in your own.

Ask yourself: "How far *is* this my problem at all? In what respects is this my problem? Am I really being of help to the other person? Even if they are happy with what I am doing, is it really in their best long term interests? Is there anything in my own life that I am *avoiding* as a result of bothering so much about the other person? If this is not really my problem, then what *is* my problem right now? And what do I need to do about it?"

9. I am waiting for **someone else** to come along and solve my problem for me!

Here is the opposite pattern of behaviour to that described in '8' above, and the one pattern fits, hand in glove, with the other. You can play the role of passive, helpless person if you like; and you *may* find someone who is prepared to play the role of rescuer or saviour. In the short run this will seem wonderful, because you no longer need to face up to your own responsibilities. Instead, you can let the other person make all the decisions for you.

In the longer run, though, this cosy arrangement comes unstuck for two reasons. First, you will generally find that the other person is not so brilliant after all at solving all your problems for you to your own satisfaction; and you will start to feel frustrated and resentful. Secondly, your refusal to stand on your own feet will lead you to forget how to do this, so that you will become less and less competent at doing things for yourself.

Thus you will become more dependent on the other person at the same time as you get disillusioned about their *ability* to rescue you. To make matters worse, your own self-confidence and self-esteem will diminish as you realise that you have forgotten how to stand up for yourself.

So, the passive person who is found by his or her rescuer ends up disillusioned and (even more) passive and helpless. And the passive person who is *not* 'rescued'? (S)he goes on waiting and waiting and hoping that the fairy prince or princess, or expert or saviour or magician will appear. And, all the time the problem is likely to get worse, with new problems piling up; and the 'helpless' person gets more and more in the habit of staying helpless and increasingly scared of facing up to the (ever-growing) pile of problems.

Clearly this is no way of dealing with a problem, and the sooner we realise this, the easier it is to make some changes and take some action.

10. I **wait** until the last minute before I tackle a problem.

⋆ Do you wait until your problem has become an emergency or, at the very least, *extremely urgent* before you will be bothered to do anything about it?

⋆ Do you wait until the problem has become a real *crisis* before you tackle it?

⋆ When the problem has become a crisis, do you get tense and in a panic about it?

⋆ Is panic and extreme tension the only means you have of overcoming your inertia and 'exhaustion'?

⋆ Do you then rush into it and, one way or another, get it sorted out – at the eleventh hour and fifty-ninth minute?

There are some really big 'payoffs' to this sort of behaviour. By waiting until we are in a panic, we can avoid facing up to our fatigue and inertia and thus avoid finding out why we feel like this. Sudden exhaustion at the thought of facing up to a problem is not genuine tiredness. But we can find it painful to deal with the real reasons for our 'fatigue'. We often prefer to avoid looking at, and dealing with, this 'exhaustion'.

Instead, we can simply wait until all the alarm bells are ringing and then, when we are really tense and anxious, the fatigue seems to disappear all by itself and we get on with the job without any sort of internal conflict about it. We no longer need to ask; "do I really want to do this, and does this really need to be done?" We just go to it. Now that it has become an emergency there is no problem for us in tackling it!

There is another payoff: By putting things off until the last minute we provide ourselves with a bit of drama. We introduce into our lives the kind of excitement involved in an action-movie, where we ask "Will he – won't he succeed?" For those of us who feel that our lives are basically too dull and humdrum, this excitement gives us a sense of importance, at least for a little while. Quite often, in fact, people will say "I can't stop, I must rush" as if this showed, not that they were incompetent and inefficient, but they were terribly busy and therefore terribly important people!

And so there are big payoffs in putting things off until the last minute. But there are even bigger snags! We rush and scramble at the problem, and so we tend to make many mistakes that could have otherwise been avoided. We get ourselves into a tense and anxious state and this is very exhausting and debilitating. Moreover, when we are putting things off and delaying for too long, we usually have an underlying sense of unease and guilt, because we suspect, quite rightly, that we are not dealing with our problems very adequately, and that we could, and should, be making a better job of things.

Again, much of the remedy for this is fairly obvious once you are reasonably well aware of what it is you are doing. We need to listen more carefully to our own assessments of what needs to be done and get on with it sooner, rather than waiting until the last moment (which is always the easy way out).

11. I let **short-term comfort** triumph over my longer-term well-being.

We tend to opt for short-term comfort rather than longer-term well-being because we don't look much beyond our own noses! If we were to look further ahead in front of us, and get a clearer picture in our minds of what will serve us best in the longer term, we would find it much easier to take action. Also it is helpful to compare the short-term picture with the (much worse) image of how things will be if we always delay. We can find all the motivation we need to behave more constructively and effectively if we only divert our gaze from the immediate present and re-focus so that we see the precipice that we are slipping down.

People can look back on their lives and sometimes ask, "How on earth did I get myself into that mess?" The answer, commonly, is that they did it by never looking more than two or three steps ahead of themselves. What looked like the easiest and most comfortable path then turned out to be an extremely dangerous and destructive option.

Come to think of it, this is how hunters set traps for many animals. The victim scents the bait that is immediately in front of it and doesn't examine the longer term costs of biting on the hook or jumping into the cage! And so short-term happiness, in the form of a good meal, is obtained at the expense of real freedom. Many of us give up our own freedom in the same way!

Having said that, there are people with another kind of personality who do the opposite. They are not slaves of short-term comfort, but instead they become the prisoners of their long-term plans. In other words, they are so obsessed with the longer-term, and so used to putting off present pleasures for future gains that they forget about how to live and how to enjoy themselves in the present. Instead, they spend their entire lives 'living for the future'.

If you go to this extreme, you will find that you won't have much of a life at all. For, although we can try to live *for* the future we cannot live in the future (or the past for that matter). The only time we can live is here and now; but some people become so obsessed with investing for future dividends that they never find themselves able to enjoy the results of the earlier sacrifices that they have made. Indeed, such sacrifices, such endless deferral of pleasure, becomes the only form of enjoyment that remains.

12. I fear that, if I tackle this problem, I will be faced with **even worse** problems which will have to be dealt with next.

Such fear can occur in many situations; particularly with problems about personal relationships. People will avoid looking at a certain 'issue' that they have with, say, their partner, because they fear that it will be like opening 'Pandora's Box'. They imagine that a great swarm of dreadful and insoluble problems will pour out all over them and smother them.

Sadly, there *is* a risk that this will occur among people who have for a long time been *repressing* hostile feelings. All too easily a large accumulation of 'unfinished business' can build up; all manner of resentments, hurts, and irritations that have never been brought to the surface and discussed and examined in an atmosphere of goodwill.

We can then start to feel like an unstable, explosive and dangerous 'powder keg' of tension and anger. We become reluctant to face up to even trivial disagreements that we have with another person for fear that this will spark off all the other accumulated resentments. We sense, rightly, that if we explode at the other person with all of these resentments, then it will probably be harmful and destructive to ourselves and others.

Clearly, it is desirable to try to avoid letting unresolved tensions build up in the first place, and discuss these with those concerned, in an atmosphere of mutual respect and toleration. However, when resentment and tension *has* already built up, it is very important to try to let out some of these tensions without having them all burst out at once. It is easier said than done; and more will be said about this elsewhere. Unless we try to release some of our tension, we will suffer from the effects of bottled up anger, and there is a likelihood that, at some time, we will explode with rage as still more niggling irritations build up.

Fear of what might happen next after we have dealt with a particular problem is quite common, and it is quite often difficult to root it out because, in order to really hide away from our fears, we avoid even facing that we *have* them.

We may be afraid of some more serious problem that might follow on from the present one, or which we will discover to lie under the surface of our present difficulties. We may fear that we will discover something unpleasant about ourselves, about our relationship with another, or about another person.

And so it is that, sometimes, we hang on to superficial, trivial issues which are really just *symptoms* of a more important underlying problem. For example, a couple might argue about minor resentments when the underlying reason is the (major) concern that they are losing interest in each other.

Sometimes, on the other hand, we are scared of what might *not* happen after we have dealt with a problem. We may be scared that there might not be enough to do when we have finished with our present task. Fear of boredom, of emptiness, of a vacuum, with a sense of meaninglessness and purposelessness that accompanies it, is very real for many of us. And so we will cling on to even very painful and unpleasant dramas and difficulties rather than have nothing at all.

We can at times become quite attached to our problems, and begin to see them as a part of who we are. We then might spend years pretending to try to deal with our problems, but in fact we would sorely miss them if they were ever finally tackled; and so we make sure that these problems hang around us indefinitely!

For example, we might enjoy feeling that we are a victim, or a martyr, or righteous, outraged, angry, tense, depressed, and so on. If these qualities and 'problems' come to be seen as a part of our identity, then we will be as reluctant to lose them as we would be to lose a limb. The 'mystery', the 'vacuum', the 'unknown' that might follow on if we were to finish with the problems we know and love can sometimes seem more scary than our present set of 'terrible' problems. And so we become stuck.

Such behaviour explains Parkinson's Law, which states that "work expands to fill the time available". If we suspect that there is dead or empty time lurking in the future, then we will even hang on to our present difficulties and tragedies, rather than be faced with 'nothing'!

Most of us will have a number of dilemmas and unsolved problems in our lives that we are simply fidgeting with. If we are more honest with ourselves, we will admit that *we already know* what needs to be done; we are simply afraid to take action, or we are reluctant to admit that our (non-ideal) solution really is the best answer that we are likely to find.

Quite frequently, then, we can pretend to ourselves that we haven't got an answer – when in fact we have! And on other occasions, we will do the opposite; and pretend that we *have* the answer – when in fact we haven't!

13. I would tackle this problem more effectively if I was more **persistent** with it.

* Do you expect that every problem will 'yield' to your efforts straightaway? Or are you willing to expect and cope with set-backs, 'failures', and disappointments?

* Do you want to be free of all surprises, distractions, inner doubts, conflicts, disillusionment and despair? Or are you prepared to accept that reality will, more often than not, turn out to be rather different from your plans and ideals?

* Do you give up completely as soon as you find that 'the wind is no longer blowing fair behind you'?

Persistence does not have to be, and works best when it is not, a violent, tension-making, super-energetic, dramatic and stormy process of hammering furiously head-on against our difficulties. It is more often successful if it is quiet, tentative, patient, gentle, relaxed, open-minded, tolerant, forgiving and peaceful. With persistence, we can gently and firmly bring ourselves back to the task in hand, whatever surprise discoveries we may find.

Unnecessary tension, heaving, fussing and gritting of teeth simply become distractions and a useless waste of energy that gets in the way of our achieving our goals. It is more useful if we approach our task with grace, peace and an economy of effort. If we dance with and explore the problem rather than struggle, battle and fight with it. In this way we can remain persistent with it for a very long time without exhausting ourselves in the process, so that we avoid becoming tired, burnt out and bitter.

In order to learn to be more persistent, we need to master many of the other skills examined throughout this book. In particular, we need to know how to relax (section fifty-five) and deal with our own internal conflicts (section fifty-six).

14. I would cope better if I was more willing to **face up** to and learn from my fears.

If we keep on avoiding and running away from our fears, then we cannot learn from them and cannot judge if they should be heeded or over-ruled. A person who is always letting her fears get on top of her will never take on any task or challenge that involves the slightest risk. Since most worthwhile challenges involve some sort of risk, (s)he will not take much on and will therefore never feel very fulfilled. Instead, (s)he will always (rightly) suspect that she is not making much use of her potential, and will feel rather stale, jaded, guilty and somewhat irritated with herself.

To make matters worse, a fear that is never faced tends to seem larger and more threatening than it really is, and so a person who constantly avoids and runs away from fear nonetheless tends always to be haunted by these phantoms.

And so it is a mistake to keep on running away from our fears, since they will go on chasing us and grow ever larger. Nonetheless, we do need to respect them and pay attention to the warnings that we give ourselves. Cowardice is no solution; but neither is masochism!... Sometimes we will decide that it *is* sensible to follow the advice of our fears and avoid the risks and dangers that scare us. After all, the costs of heroism can sometimes be greater than the benefits – to ourselves or anyone else.

Regardless of whether or not we act upon, or over-rule, our fear, there is no need for us to be harsh on ourselves. If we attack or repress our fears; they are likely to 'go underground' yet remain as persistent and painful as ever. We may push them out of awareness; but they will still be present in us. And because we are not facing up to them, they are likely, as long shadows, to seem larger and more threatening than they really are.

We may sometimes feel guilty because we are afraid; but if our guilt is harsh and unforgiving then we will have created yet another source of useless suffering for ourselves! To feel guilty about feeling fearful is often just one more distraction.

Instead, why not acknowledge it when we really are afraid, and learn from the experience? We can then, if we wish, go ahead with the task that scares us, *despite* our fear. In other words we can (respectfully) over-rule our fear rather than try to repress and overcome it.

Fear is not something that we have to fight. It is, as it were, one of our 'counsellors' and 'advisers', that we listen to before taking action, but whose advice we do not always have to heed.

The courageous person is not the one who knows no fear. Rather, she knows that she is afraid, but carries on with what she intends to do all the same. After all, if you really were not afraid to do something and really had managed to make the fear disappear then you would no longer *need* any courage!

Fear is not an enemy, nuisance, obstacle, evil, hindrance, or source of shame. On the contrary, it is, like any other feeling, a potentially useful adviser/guide/trusty-friend/counsellor/early-warning system that we will sometimes heed and sometimes over-rule.

Regardless of whether we heed our fears or over-rule them, we will be better off if we pay attention to them with appropriate respect and thanks.

15. I would tackle the problem more effectively if I was more **decisive**.

"I am firm and decisive...
You are stubborn...
He is pig-headed!"
... in other words, it can very much depend on your point of view as to whether or not someone is being 'decisive', and there is no simple formula that will tell you whether or not your opinion is 'right'. Clearly we can be too rigid, and insist on taking decisions prematurely. All too often we then cling on stubbornly to these – regardless of the evidence against us.

At the other extreme, we can swing around in our views like a weather-vane, so much so that no one can have confidence that we will ever stick to any decision we have made. Instead, we will change our views with every slight influence and opinion that is presented. Often we will do this because we are lacking in confidence and self-esteem, and are busy trying to please everyone. This sort of behaviour eventually pleases no one, so that by such dithering we end up losing everyone's respect.

16. I run into difficulties with problems because I am basically **lazy!**...

This is a very common, and seemingly 'commonsense' term. And yet what precisely, or even imprecisely, does it mean? The word 'laziness' is, I think, used as a (much too) vague umbrella-term that has a wide variety of possible meanings. For example, a person accused of laziness might be:

a. Putting short-term comfort before longer-term well-being, by failing to take the longer view. (See section eleven.)

b. Letting (known or unknown) fears triumph over action. (Section fourteen.)

c. Suffering from low self-esteem and a general lack of confidence, which might show itself as 'fatigue'. (Section nineteen.)

d. Hoping that the problem will go away all by itself. (Section five.)

e. Hoping that someone else will solve the problem. (Section nine.)

f. Feeling scared of what might lie behind a problem. (Section twelve.)

There are many, quite different, patterns of behaviour that can lie at the root of laziness. One of the aims of this book, in fact, is to provide a much sharper focus on what is described as the laziness of people so that you can see more clearly and precisely what is actually going on. Laziness is not a description that in itself explains why we behave as we do.

Commonly, the lazy person feels 'just too tired' to face the problem. It is fascinating to notice the wide variety of circumstances where we can suddenly find ourselves overcome with exhaustion! Whenever we are faced with a problem that, for whatever reason, we don't wish to look at, we can suddenly feel 'exhausted'. Similarly, whenever unwanted feelings, thoughts and wishes loom up inside us, or we are faced with unwanted circumstances or people, we will sometimes use 'fatigue' as a way of driving them all away.

In fact, of course, this physical exhaustion is not genuine, and this is clear to see, because as soon as the threatening problem/person/circumstance disappears we suddenly find that we are no longer tired; especially if something else comes along that actually attracts and excites us!

17. I am not tackling this problem because I am **pessimistic** about my chances of not being able to deal with it . . .

Pessimism seems very common these days; about ourselves and what we can do as individuals, and about what people as a whole can achieve. Individuals and whole cultures can begin at the one extreme of being overly optimistic and idealistic about what is possible; and later, in reaction, swing to the other extreme of becoming excessively gloomy and depressive. And so for example, in the Nineteen Sixties, many young people thought that 'Utopia' could be brought about within a lifetime if we worked at it, whereas in the Nineteen Eighties (and Nineties?) the motif often tends to be "we've tried it all before and it doesn't work!"

The trouble is that, when you take a really pessimistic view about yourself and what you can do, you are likely to find that your gloomy predictions come true! You don't believe that you can achieve anything; it looks like there is no point in trying, and so you don't try. There seems to be nothing to hope for and get excited and enthusiastic about, and so you remain feeling hopeless, bored, jaded, weary, stale and exhausted. You have a low opinion of yourself and, because you don't try to do anything and therefore fail to achieve anything, you consider that, yet again, your low opinion about yourself has been more than amply justified. A vicious cycle.

The remedy, of course, is to take some positive action *despite* the fact that you feel pessimistic. With even tiny amounts of success you will find that you can begin to break out of the vicious cycle, and build up a more positive sequence of small successes encouraging more efforts leading to further achievements. See also section twelve.

Problems arising from a lack of LOVE:

18. I would benefit if I could find someone to **talk** to about this problem.

Are you the sort of person who tries to 'go it alone' all the time? Self-sufficiency can be fine up to a point; but do you consider it to be a weakness to make good use of advice, information and emotional support from others? O.K., so not all the help we receive is necessarily helpful, even when it is well intended; and we can sometimes wish that others would spare us their advice! Indeed, the best kind of support often comes not so much from the ideas, opinions and advice of others, but simply from their willingness to listen and take an interest.

Have you noticed how the very act of talking about a problem with someone else can help you to get a much clearer perspective on your doubts, fears and conflicts; and allow you to see what you want to do next? Others can be of great service if they just listen; without necessarily giving us any advice at all. We may well not need any more advice, since there is a glut of this in any case, and it can sometimes prevent us from sorting out what we think about the problem.

How to get this opportunity to talk with others though? It is not always easy because not everyone is a particularly good listener! Nonetheless, it's well worth looking around to see who might be able to help; it is not a weakness to get this kind of support from others; in fact it requires a certain amount of *strength*, since it involves putting your trust in others, and relying on them to not misuse or exploit your confiding in them.

It is not guaranteed, of course, but others are rather more likely to be willing to listen and to take a genuine interest in your problems if you show a real interest in *them*!

19. I need to trust myself more and have more **confidence** in my ability to deal with this problem. I am competent but not sufficiently confident!

The magic of confidence! If only we had more of it! Others can seem so much more confident than we are. "How do they do it?" we ask ourselves. "If they only knew how lacking in confidence I was; I must make sure that they don't find out about the real, unconfident, me; I must put on a good show."

What *is* the secret of confidence? Is there a secret at all? How do we become, or fail to become, more confident?

To put it (very) crudely, there are three kinds of people: those who obviously lack confidence; those who *seem* to be confident but who are not; and those who genuinely *are* confident. I suspect that there are (relatively) few in the latter category!

The interesting case is that large group who put on a good show of being self-assured, but who are far less confident than they pretend. Take, for example, the dominating ego-maniac who has always got to achieve, succeed, be the best, beat the rest, compete frantically *against* others, make as much as possible 'me-and-mine'. Does this style of behaviour indicate confidence? Is it a genuinely confident person who is always having to prove how good and successful he is? And is it confidence that demands that we run away from our faults, failings, fears, and foibles; and always present our best side to others? Surely not.

Of course we will all prefer to succeed and achieve our ideals; but, so often, we make the mistake of insisting that we 'should' be successful, and feeling that it is a disaster if we fail. All too commonly, we develop a manic need to prove how good we are, not because we have such a high opinion of ourselves, but, on the contrary, because we think so *little* of ourselves. For so many of us, the underlying thought is that . . . "If people really knew me they would all back off in shock and horror and run away!" or, "I could never look anyone in the face if they discovered my guilty secrets, failures, fears and conflicts; I would be so ashamed!" And so the constant need to keep proving that we really are O.K.

Such behaviour can become a real treadmill for us. If we fail then our self-esteem falls still further, and we think; "Well, that just *proves* that I'm no good!" But if we succeed, this provides little respite, since we 'have to' keep on 'proving' that we still are as good as our last great achievement. Moreover, there is the fear that we might never be able to better or equal our last success; that underneath we are still no good really, and that sooner or later we will fail and/or someone else will steal ahead of us and take our place.

The Rat Race world is very much the result of large numbers of us needing to prove how 'great' we are, as a result of our underlying fear and doubt. And what a tiresome, tension-making, unfriendly world it is where so many people are trying so hard to be special all the time; to leave their own unique mark; to be immortal. We can so easily become addicted to the idea of success. We come to believe that, unless we have it, we are doomed; or, were we to lose it, it would be a catastrophe.

This obsession with success is a major obstacle to people developing confidence in themselves. Probably the main reason why people do not often achieve their full potential is not that they lack intelligence or motivation, but that they are just too concerned to get everything right and to do everything really well.

You want to stop a child learning to read? Tell her that it's incredibly important that she learn, that others are doing better than she is and that she really ought to worry about this. You want to stop yourself taking on a new job, meeting new people, trying something new? Tell yourself that it's *terrible* that you might make mistakes; horrible that you are less skilled than others, and unbearably painful that you are a long way from achieving your ideals!

In this way you can get really worried about not being as good as you would like, about making mistakes, being rejected, getting less than you want. And, as a result of this, you can get very self-preoccupied and self-obsessed, tense, sick and weary. This will very effectively prevent you from learning the things you so much want to learn, and you may very well give up altogether. Certainly, whatever you *do* learn will be done with far more worry and tension than necessary and your learning will be far less rapid, effective and efficient than it could have been.

It is really easy to teach someone who is very bright; not so much because they are very intelligent, but because they are generally being told every day how much better they are than everyone else. Such experience is very rewarding for them, and is an easy way of building up confidence. Much more valuable is to build up people's confidence regardless of whether or not they are doing well.

Of course it is good to wish, and learn how, to succeed. An even greater challenge, though, is to know how to 'fail' and to see it, not as a disaster, but as a golden opportunity to learn. After all, if events always go according to plan we can easily become smug, sleepy and complacent. When they don't, we have a real chance of learning something new.

Moreover, if we can merely *prefer* rather than insist upon success, then every stage of learning can become enjoyable, and our confidence does not have to depend on our always 'winning' and succeeding. In this way we can be confident without being a hostage to circumstances (which quite often will not 'dance to our tune' in the way we would like). Consequently, we can enjoy both the achievement and the (much longer) process of trying to get there. We can enjoy it if we succeed and become a master of the task we have set ourselves; and we can also enjoy just being mediocre, a beginner, someone who is making plenty of mistakes.

Clearly, if you can be confident only after you have really succeeded in all the things you set out to do, then most of us are doomed to a life of self-doubt, unease and low self-esteem. We will be unable to like, trust, respect and have confidence in ourselves! In fact, of course, we don't have to do 'great things' in order to become confident: *Confidence is not about being successful and super all the time; it's about feeling O.K. and accepting yourself . . . as you are!*

So often we say to ourselves "I could be a really confident, relaxed, peaceful person, and could really like myself, *if only* I could get myself and my life properly straightened out". Let's be quite clear about it, we are never going to get everything sorted out! Our ideals are always going to be a good way ahead of the reality in our lives. That's how it is with ideals!

Society has, I think, become rather too obsessed with success, celebrity, fame, superlative achievements and all the ballyhoo that surrounds it. Why on earth does it have to be so important that we be wonderful all the time? Most people, by definition, are going to be 'in the middle of the pack', and some of us will find that in some respects we are really quite backward and 'retarded'! Does this mean that everyone, bar the top few percent, must feel badly about themselves and lack the confidence to really do their best? Surely not! It really is a poor state of affairs if we can't feel good and confident about being – well, ordinary.

Being ordinary ought, I think, to be our new great challenge. It's more important, really, than flying off into space. And, you know, to make a half decent job of ordinariness would be really rather *extra*ordinary! After all, the commonest thing that most people want to be is *special* . . . because, sadly, they don't realise that they are already special just by being themselves.

People often think that it is the arrogant person who has too high an opinion of herself and the humble person who is too apologetic and lacking in confidence. In fact it is the other way round! True humility requires you to have the confidence to face yourself as you really are. Whereas, arrogance struts around in order to hide an underlying lack of confidence!

It is low self-esteem and a lack of real confidence that underlies all the pride, posturing, power struggles and ego-battles that we see all around us – with so many people feeling the need to 'prove' themselves.

Why do you have to prove yourself? Why do you have to be better than others? Why do you need so much praise and recognition? Because underneath it all you feel inadequate, un-confident, no good, unworthy, and guilty. People try to 'colonise' other people, and the world around them, not because they feel good about themselves, but because they feel insecure, in-significant, threatened and unsafe. In the short run, we can mask our sense of insignificance by 'victories' and 'achievements'. But however much you get and are, you always remain a tiny, helpless speck in comparison with the vastness of Space and Time around you. And, until you can come to terms with this and see that you are both Absolutely important and relatively insignificant, the underlying insecurity remains.

We tend to think that the strong person is the one who is loud and domineering, aggressive, highly armed and armoured, well defended and able to hit, or hit back, hard. The person who has humility, who is open, open-minded, unaggressive and nondefensive we see as weak and naive.

Yet, what is it that underlies all the muscle-armour and lack of emotion of the 'strong' person? Well, *fear*, of course! And a fear that is not even recognised and acknowledged. The (so-called) 'strong' person is always considering himself to be in potentially hostile territory, so that he 'has to' be on his guard all the time. Again, it is all posture and pretense, and the strength, confidence and self-respect would be all the greater if he was able to weep, shiver with fear, express his worries and doubts and conflicts, and do all this without feeling that he was 'less' of a person. Because, in fact, he would be 'more of' a person; the 'more' being all those hidden away fears, tears, doubts and failings that were now, at last, being released!

Real strength is required to face ourselves as we really are and to be open to the criticisms of others. Great courage is needed if we are to do all this without feeling that we have to defend ourselves or believing that we are placed in disgrace and at a disadvantage as a result of our human weaknesses.

20. I am too concerned about the **views of others**.

Unless you are exceptionally naive about, or indifferent to, other people you are bound to take a very great interest in what (some) others think of you. And so, inevitably and rightly, you will sometimes try to imagine how you appear from the point of view of friends, colleagues and acquaintances who matter to you; and to strangers whom you would like to impress.

However, for as long as we are trying to put ourselves into other people's shoes, we are not able to give our full attention to the problem in hand; and so worrying about how we are seen by others is bound to be a distraction. Moreover, worrying too much about what others might think of us, does not ultimately lead them to respect us. On the contrary, people tend to become rather contemptuous of the person who tries too hard to please and who is too much like a doormat. In any case, it is impossible to please everyone, because people will not agree about what they want from you, and each is quite capable of changing his mind from day to day about what (s)he wants from you!

Often we bother too much about how we appear to others because of our own insecurity; and this generally arises from low self-esteem. The result is that we become too preoccupied in 'putting on a show' for others; pretending to be someone we are not! This leads to chronic unease and excessive concern about how we are seen, because we worry that we will be found out; that others will see through our performance and pretence.

If we are to do well with the problem before us, we need to put our minds to that and that alone, and not waste time thinking about what others might think, or worrying about whether we will achieve our ideals, or fretting about how terrible it would be if we 'failed'.

And when we notice that we are *not* paying attention, we would be wise to bring ourselves back, gently and firmly, to the task we have set ourselves; without distracting ourselves further with excessive worry or irritation with ourselves for falling prey to distractions. After all, if you allow yourself to be distracted, it does you no good to distract yourself still further with tension, regret, worry and self-punishment!

21. I would tackle some problems more effectively if I was more **tolerant** and forgiving of myself and others.

When people talk about problems and ways of solving them, they tend to see this as a technical matter involving appropriate skills and information. But this is by no means all that may be involved.

Often, we fail to deal with our problems very effectively, and get ourselves into unnecessary difficulties, not because of a lack of knowledge and skill, but because of our basic *attitudes* and the moral position we take in relation to ourselves and others.

For example, if we are not prepared to have some reasonable *toleration* of mistakes, failings and weaknesses, then we will 'cook' ourselves into a debilitating anger, or tension, or despair, or depression about ourselves, other people and our problems generally. This can have an enormously destructive effect on our ability to tackle the problem, quite apart from destroying our physical and mental well-being.

We all dislike and regret much of our own and other people's behaviour; mistakes, errors of judgement and morally shabby actions and attitudes are common enough! We can, and should, feel due regret; and genuinely resolve to learn from our mistakes. But we then need to be able to move on to something new, and not stay stuck with endless recriminations of ourselves or others. Such a lack of forgiveness prevents us from properly learning from our mistakes: We are so busy chastising ourselves that we don't put into practice what we have learned from the errors we have made!

It is much easier, of course, to imagine that the problem is 'out there' and due to the 'trials and tribulations' thrust upon us by the outside world. Quite often, though, the problem comes from within ourselves and so, for example, can arise simply from our *lack of forgiveness*!

However, it's no good pretending to be more forgiving than we really are, or in pretending that we are not angry, irritated or even outraged at other people's behaviour – and our own! Forgiveness does not mean that you become a spineless doormat in relation to others. It means that you eventually let go of angry feelings, so that you prevent them becoming destructive to all concerned. As usual, there is no simple formula, or 'court of arbitration', that will tell you when particular feelings, thoughts or actions have moved on from being useful, constructive and supportive to being useless, destructive and undermining!

Perhaps the most destructive behaviour in relation to forgiveness is the kind of pseudo-forgiveness where the person *says* "I forgive you", but actually *means* "I forgive you in order to show what a fine person I am and in order to get you to feel even more guilty, inadequate and unworthy than you do now".

We have received real forgiveness from others when we feel that it allows us to forgive ourselves. In this way, everyone is released and renewed. Pseudo-forms of forgiveness are simply new devices to manipulate and undermine. Such false forms of forgiveness are not designed to be of help to others; they are essentially attempts to invest in one's own spiritual well-being. Beneath the (appearance of) forgiveness on the part of the pseudo-moral manipulator, there is an underlying malevolence and an unwarranted sense of superiority.

22. I need to be more compassionate and understanding of others.

We can be so keen to blame and judge ourselves and others; and clearly it *is* appropriate at times to make such judgements, although blaming is too often an irresponsible process of looking for the failings and faults elsewhere while ignoring our own!

Far more useful and important than blame, though, is to try to *understand why* we, or others, have behaved in the way we did. We may not like what happened; there are, however, always reasons for people's behaviour and, if we are to act wisely, it is important for us to try to find out just what these reasons are. It is not enough to say "There was no excuse for this!" Maybe the behaviour was not morally excusable, but, to repeat, there must have been a reason for it!

As we go deeper and deeper into the reasons, we learn more and more about the conflicts, fears, doubts, worries, hopes, dreams and attitudes of a person; and it tends to happen that the more we understand a person the more we are able to find compassion for him or her. We start to see, not only the destructive tendencies in the person, but also their potential capacity to be constructive, creative, loving and benevolent.

Inevitably, this potential is never fully realised in any of us. But once we become more aware that it is there we become more conscious of the tragic dimensions of life, and less concerned to judge and blame. We can then become more effective, and find some inner peace. It can be very painful and destructive to hold in our hearts too much judgement, condemnation and blame of ourselves or others; on the other hand, when we can feel grief at the tragedies of lost opportunity that befall us all, the release of such feelings can help us see once again the joys of life and come to terms with its limitations and frustrations.

Compassion, like all the other 'virtues' is not just some 'worthy' and difficult to achieve state of living that we 'ought' to achieve because it is one of our moral principles; it is also good for our health and makes us more effective in dealing with our problems!

23.... more **friendly** and affectionate.

Needless to say, it is much easier to be friendly and affectionate towards people we like and agree with than with those whom we dislike and who don't share our opinions; but is it naive and impossibly idealistic to see how far we can be more generally friendly towards people?

We can certainly be too naively trusting of others, since exploitation and aggression are real enough! But so often we can spend too much time being suspicious of people, and then we fail to be aware of the possible good in them. The very process of seeing the potential for good in others can help to bring it out, and, similarly, if we look too hard for betrayal, failure and weakness in others we are more likely to find thoughts turning to realities! Furthermore, the more we feel hostile towards, at odds with, and defended against, others, the more tense, uneasy, uncomfortable and ineffective we will tend to be. Better then, to keep these feelings to the absolute minimum necessary to take care of ourselves, rather than look for trouble when it may not be there.

For example, suppose you are unhappy with something you have bought at a shop, and wish to take it back and get it changed. So often, people go into such a situation armed and 'armoured' with righteous indignation, a tough, aggressive and hostile approach, and ready to try to ridicule and undermine the other person if they don't quickly exchange the goods. The whole business is seen in Win-Lose terms. It is a 'battle', a 'struggle', a 'contest', in which you are pitting your wits and skills against the other person.

And what is the result? Well, the 'opponent' is much more likely to take up a defensive posture, and will, like you, be evasive, devious, manipulative, aggressive and dishonest if any of these tactics look as though they will be likely to help him 'win'. Depending on the ground you are battling on, and your relative skills in fighting, you will either win or lose. But look at the price you are paying either way.

If you 'win', then you will have made for yourself a resentful enemy who will always be looking for a way of getting back at you, and who you will need to be all the more wary of. And if you 'lose', then you yourself will feel sullen and hostile, and anxious to see if you can get even with the other person at some later stage.

Some might say that, however painful and uncomfortable all this might be, there is no alternative, and that therefore you might as well be a winner in the Rat Race rather than a loser. Yet there *is* an alternative; and it does not involve pretending that we can, or should, abolish all conflict between people. Rather, this alternative approach consists of seeing how far we can manage our conflicts and disagreements with others with as much goodwill, mutual respect, openness and willingness to hear the other person's point of view as we can possibly muster.

In this way, the aim is no longer to 'win' or to 'lose'; it consists of seeing to what extent we can find a compromise that everyone can genuinely accept, that does not involve violating anyone's integrity, and that shows respect and concern for everyone's point of view. This is not always easy to achieve! When, though, we do manage to achieve it, we come away from a conflict with everyone's sense of self-esteem *enhanced* rather than damaged and this is a much more satisfying experience than mere victory over others.

We may feel a certain destructive kind of satisfaction when we have successfully outmanouvered, or bullied, or undermined another person. But this kind of lonely, armoured destructiveness is nothing like so fulfilling as the feelings we have when we have encouraged, respected, and supported another person. Moreover, if we can manage to be friendly and supportive with others, we are more likely to get support, respect and encouragement from them. When we 'go to war' with other people then, no matter how great our victory, there is a bitter taste in the mouth, and a great deal of pain and insecurity at the thought of their resentment, anger and dreams of revenge.

24. . . . more **respectful** of others.

If we fail to have respect for others, how can we be of use to them, and how can we believe in and benefit from what they can offer us? Without respect for others, we face our problems alone; and without respect for ourselves we cannot trust ourselves to cope either alone or with the help of others.

Respect, then, both of ourselves and others, is a crucial part of life, not just as an abstract moral principle, but as an important influence on whether or not we will be able to deal with our problems successfully!

What is it that we respect? So often, we can find that we are being respectful of the mere superficialities of life; the status symbols, power obsessions, and ego-centred 'victories' of ourselves or others. This is not a genuine respect, but a narrow pride in ourselves, or a craven attempt to curry favour from others more powerful than we are. Underlying such ego-centred strategems is a lack of respect and a lack of confidence and trust in ourselves as we really are, with all our 'failings' and weaknesses.

With a genuine respect in ourselves and others, we can face

and deal with each other as we really are, and not just with our dreams or ideals. Respect goes with a genuine humility rather than with excessive pride; since this is always the result of wilful self-deception. We know in our hearts that we are never so wonderful as we can pretend; and the pretence is itself the result of a refusal to face our limitations and weaknesses, through a lack of love and respect for ourselves.

25. I need to be less **guilty** and ashamed of myself.

Do you sometimes find that, the minute you try to take some action about a problem, you start moaning away to yourself that you are no good, that you should have started earlier, that you are not functioning as well as you should, that you should be feeling really badly about yourself?

Such thinking, of course, has a very undermining effect on our self-confidence and self-esteem, which leads us to retreat still further away from the problem rather than put ourselves into it heart and soul. And so a vicious cycle develops where I say to myself:

"I'm no good; and facing this is painful, so I'll withdraw from the problem. I've withdrawn from facing up to the problem, and so this proves, yet again, that I'm no good."

The negative thinking creates still more negative thinking; and the negative prophecies become self-fulfilling. In other words, you can 'beat yourself up' about how bad you are, and the result is that you have less confidence to approach the problem. Then, because you have retreated from facing up to the problem, you lash yourself some more. Or: We begin by being too ashamed to face the problem, and then, because we have not faced it, we feel ashamed about that as well!

In order to deal adequately with this pattern of behaviour, we need to understand the important role that shame and guilt play in our lives; and we need to learn to distinguish between *destructive* and *constructive* uses of guilt; or, to put it another way, between 'useful' and 'useless' guilt.

Let us remember that guilt does very often serve a useful purpose. After all, if you never feel guilty about anything, how could you ever achieve your ideals, abide by your rules, live up to your values, give meaning to your beliefs and keep on target with your aims? If you never felt regret when you strayed from the direction you had set yourself, instead remaining as content as ever, then you would have no incentive or motivation to stick to your path. We keep to the goals we have set ourselves because we feel better about doing so; but, in order to feel 'better', there has to be the possibility of feeling 'worse'.

Feelings of guilt function like the rudder on a ship. When it goes off course, the rudder can be used gently and firmly to correct matters. Complete freedom from such guilt would indeed leave us adrift like a ship without a rudder, at the mercy of any passing whim and fancy. If we never felt guilty, we would never be free to make choices and *stick* to them (and holding fast to one's choice despite passing fancies is quite essential if 'choice' is to have any meaning!). *Freedom* from guilt would enslave us, leaving us unable to take a perspective on the ever changing ripples of thought and feeling that are the inevitable buffeting of experience.

We are probably all of us, with the possible exception of the occasional psychopath, prey to our guilty feelings. We all, as it were, have inside us a 'voice of conscience' that 'rewards' us with a sense of satisfaction when we have done well, and which 'punishes' us with feelings of remorse, regret, tension, sadness, shame, frustration – *guilt* – when we have failed to live up to our own ideals, rules and values.

The mechanism of guilt can, however, become destructive rather than benign. A rudder on a ship is firm and gentle; and some people are lucky enough to have a voice of conscience that is like a firm and supportive friend. The trouble is that, for so many of us, our voice of conscience is like a 'harsh and domineering tyrant', and is not at all compassionate and forgiving. In other words, when we break our own rules or fail in some other way, we moan and gnash at ourselves, 'beat ourselves up', feel a strong self-dislike, even hatred, of ourselves. And, rather than say that we are (merely) 'regretful' and 'disappointed', we consider that we are 'appalled' at ourselves, and that what has happened is a 'catastrophe'!

Think about this. Do others moan at and bully you? Perhaps they do. But I doubt that they do it to you as much as you do it to yourself! In my experience, and for most people, the worst bully, the greatest nag, the most hideous, moaning, unforgiving, critical, domineering tyrant is ME – *of myself*! I think that is why we so often find it difficult to put up with the moans of others! We moan at ourselves so much and so endlessly; when others start on us as well it seems like the last straw!

So often, our consciences are tyrannical rather than friendly because too many other people, from childhood onwards, have been actively *encouraging* us to have this low opinion of ourselves. The reason? People do this in order to get you to do whatever it is that *they* want you to do. After all, if I can persuade you that you are a 'bad' person, and can get you to feel really inadequate for not fitting in with what *I* want, then you are more likely to do things my way so that you can avoid being plagued by your guilty feelings.

This kind of ploy goes on all the time. We all of us misuse guilt in order to get what we want. We pretend that our personal preferences are really moral principles and then try to get other people to feel bad if they dare to go against us. The result? Our **self-esteem**, our basic liking, acceptance and respect of ourselves, is often dangerously low.

Mind you, although others will try to get you to feel bad, you need to remember that it is you who allows them to get away with this and, after years of habit, I doubt that they are as hard on you as you are hard on yourself!

"Ah, but I deserve it! I'm such a bad person. I have to be really hard on myself, since otherwise I would go to pieces, behave terribly, abandon all my standards! I have to be a tyrant with myself because that is the only way that I can keep myself in order! I have to be cruel to be kind!"

So speaks our tyrannical conscience. But is it (are we) right about this? Does the bullying actually work very well? In my experience, the tyrannical type of conscience works very badly indeed! Because, when I am not being too tough with myself, I am likely to be going to the opposite extreme of saying "To hell with all this! I want some fun! I want some pleasure and enjoyment! I can't and won't live up to such impossibly high standards!" And then I sabotage all my previous efforts and go on some sort of 'binge'.

Do you see how this pattern works? And can you see that the more you try to push yourself to one tyrannical extreme the more you will go in for a violent and licentious backlash at the other end of the spectrum?

Too often we have been taught by others whose tone and manner was not always very kind. We tend to internalise the tone of voice we heard most often as a child and, sadly, this culture is still infested with the decadent versions of Christian teaching which preach that it is always good to feel bad, that we are all selfish, heartless, miserable swine who need to be held in check; that our natural disposition is to be unruly and destructive! Oh yes, and there is, of course, the voice at the other extreme that says "To hell with it all, do exactly what you want, there are no rules and standards, nothing matters". We have been experiencing a bit of this backlash against more Victorian ways at the present time. But each extreme position feeds off and supports the other, and we, and the culture as a whole, oscillate to and fro between such (equally destructive) extremes. (So now are we doomed to rebound back into some form of Puritanism?)

Notice the damaging effects of the low self-esteem arising from the tyrannical conscience! People think: "If others really knew me they would all run away in shock and horror, I am such a bad person. Nobody could stand me as I really am!" Such an attitude is common even within (particularly within) the ego-centric figure who seems so full of herself and who struts her way through the day. This person, too, is often having to 'prove' to herself and others that she is good, beautiful, successful, worthwhile etc. And why the constant need to achieve and prove that she is O.K.? Because, so often, at the bottom of her heart, she doesn't believe it!

Our low self-esteem, brought on by the tyrant-conscience, leads us to hide away from ourselves, and from others, all those 'bad bits' of personality that we feel too ashamed and guilty to face. Even when alone, we feel painfully guilty and uncomfortable on confronting our 'shadowy', 'wicked' self! This is one of the reasons why we are so unaware of so many of our thoughts, feelings and day-dreams and so unconscious of much of our behaviour. We avoid facing up to it, because we think that we *shouldn't* be like this!

Forgiveness, love, tolerance, acceptance begins 'at home' – with each of us facing up to ourselves as we are. For unless we can be open to, and accepting of, ourselves how can we expect to be open and accepting of others? And if there are so many parts of ourselves that we won't face up to (for fear that our conscience will make such a fuss!) then how can we learn from these buried feelings and fantasies?

Not surprising, then, that the guilt-ridden individual is burdened with all kinds of unfinished issues from the past (she never wanted to face them) and suffers from chronic anxiety and tension – the causes of which she is unaware (she would be so hard on herself if she let herself know).

The person whose conscience is a harsh and domineering tyrant will tend always to be fearful, uneasy, 'at odds with' herself, insecure, tense and restless. Because, whatever she is doing, it is not being done 'well enough' for the tyrant-conscience that is (a part of) her.

And underneath the guilt, there is likely to be a mass (mess) of other feelings that she is scared of facing (for fear of what her conscience might do); like anger, exhaustion, resentment at the whole predicament, confusion, sullenness and despair.

Even more silly; that other part of us which greatly resents our feelings, will say, "O.K. so I've felt miserable about this for so long. I've paid heavily for what I did wrong. I am now 'in credit' and can go off and make the same mistake again, then pay the (guilt) price later!"

Far from really intending to learn and change, we go round and round in the same old circles.

Nine ways of getting on top of Guilt:

1. When you find that you are moaning at and bullying yourself, try turning this harsh and bossy voice into one that is just as firm, but much more kind and forgiving. We all respond best to friendly, respectful and courteous voices and this is just as true when the voice is 'inside us' as when it is from someone else.

2. If the tone and attitude of your conscience is still harsh and

cruel, imagine that it is no longer seated in your higher self (or wherever else you place it) but, instead, shift it in your fantasy so that it would appear to be coming from some less exalted spot – like your big toe for example! It is amazing how less tyrannical your conscience seems when it is coming from your toe, or from under a pile of cushions or wherever else you might like to put it to lessen its power.

3. Alternatively, *identify* with your conscience; remember that this is **you** moaning at yourself and look at the poor victim of your bullying and see if you can be more forgiving, more kind and gentle to her. She really will respond better with a kinder voice you know.

4. If you are bothered with troubling visual images from your conscience, rather than bullying voices; (for example, perhaps you are plagued with fantasies of catastrophe, domineering individuals telling you how bad you are etc.) – see if you can change these so that they are less threatening. For instance, shrink the mental picture that you have in your 'mind's eye'; (and/or turn the sound down!); or imagine that it is just a film show you are watching; or put a funny hat on the person who is moaning at you. There are endless possibilities. The underlying principle, in dealing with our conscience, should be that we *learn* from it without being overwhelmed and assaulted by it!

5. Remember, *you* control how much guilt you feel about anything! How? Because you (and you alone) decide whether the standards you have set are too hard or too easy for you and you can change these standards any time you want. (Naturally, this has consequences that need to be weighed!) Of course, it is often difficult to decide whether we ought to try harder or give ourselves a rest, but it can be exhilarating when you remember that this decision really is in your hands. For then you can see the comical truth that guilt is not something that is thrust upon us by a demanding world, but is the result of our making demands on ourselves! We each of us control how guilty we shall feel, since we each set our own standards. If you can really take in and digest this one, it will give you more freedom than you ever thought possible.

6. There are, to repeat, two sorts of guilt; Useful Guilt and Useless Guilt. The useful variety gives us strong firm twinges at

times but is not sadistic; and so we learn and change and carry out our intentions while being tolerant and forgiving about our (inevitable) failures. The useless variety, on the other hand, gives us a very hard time, enjoys cruelty and bullying; but we don't learn or notice much and we sabotage many of the changes we are trying to make. And so, whenever you are plagued by guilty feelings ask yourself; "Is this useful or useless? What purpose is it serving? It is helping me to achieve anything?" And, if it is not helping you, deal with it, interrupt it, change it. You *can* you know!

7. If you have been a real slave to guilty feelings there may well be a kind of 'under-dog' voice in you that winges and cringes in relation to your tyrant conscience with apologies like, "I am doing my best, I'm trying really hard, I'm sorry, I really must do better next time, I'm on my knees, please forgive me!" etc. If so, it may be useful for you to put some more energy and assertiveness into this cringing part of yourself. For example, next time you moan at yourself about your endless failures, what about telling this moaning part to *$/?ß off! Let that part of you that is tired of your bullying speak up. If you can let all the parts of you speak up in this internal conflict (that we all have) then you will be more likely to make realistic decisions that you will actually be willing and able to carry out.

8. If you are plagued by others who get you to fit in with them by encouraging you to feel guilty then ask yourself: "Do I *have* to go along with other people all the time? Are their views *always* the 'right' and good ones? Do I *have to* feel guilty when I defy these 'pseudo-moralists' and arch-manipulators?" You don't you know! As soon as you see the devious game that others are playing you can begin to get yourself out of the guilt trap. It's one thing to feel guilty when you really have done something you know to be wrong or inadequate. It's quite another matter to feel bad because others are trying to undermine you. Start noticing the difference and trust yourself to be the judge of this. And, as a useful guide, remember that Guilt without Love is self-torture that serves no useful purpose!

9. Don't, for goodness sake, go to the other extreme of trying to get rid of guilt altogether! An acquaintance of mine once said: "I've plagued myself with guilt for so long. I'm absolutely sick of

it! I've decided, to hell with it, I'm never going to feel guilty about anything ever again!" This way, you 'throw the baby out with the bath water' and, for sure, you will never achieve anything that requires any sort of self-discipline, persistence, concentration and effort.

Sometimes, after all, we *should* feel guilt about what we have done, or not done; and any 'therapy' that seeks to free you from all guilt is both amoral and untherapeutic!

Decadent versions of Western Religions go in for a harsh 'Tyrant-Conscience' where suffering is seen almost as a virtue! In the East, on the other hand, the decadent form seeks to abolish guilt and suffering altogether by giving up all attachment and desire...

"Abandon all wants" is the cry, "and then you won't feel disappointed if you don't get anything. Don't try to achieve anything and thus you will be free of all guilt and regret!"

Such a policy of renunciation can actually work, and we *can* reduce guilt and other forms of suffering in this way; by letting go of all our plans, hopes and expectations. The trouble is that, in the process, we lose our personality and humanity and turn ourselves into passive cabbages! Fortunately, saner forms of Christian and Buddhist teachings are aware of these built-in dangers.

Problems arising from a lack of WISDOM:

26. I need to be more **clear** and systematic.

What do you generally do when you are faced with a problem and you don't really know how large it is? Do you tend to over-estimate or under-estimate its size? Generally speaking, in my experience, people over-estimate the problem and exaggerate how difficult it will be. In other words, an *unknown* 'threat', of unknown size, tends to be seen as a *big* threat and bigger than it really is.

The remedy is obvious. We need to find out the actual scale of the problem as soon as we can, and in this way it can be brought down to its real size, and cut up into manageable portions. Then, we can get to work to see just how we will cope with it, and the very process of doing this will tend to raise our morale and confidence and help us to get going with all the more energy and enthusiasm.

Obvious, isn't it? The trouble is we often do the *opposite*. Instead of saying:

"This seems to be a big problem, but it will probably seem smaller once I have got the measure of it." ... we say:

"This seems to be a big problem, and so I'd better keep clear of it and hope that it won't catch up on me!"

Hence, in order to avoid a bit of short-term 'discomfort', we end up with far *more* pain and suffering; with a problem that continues to haunt us and which seems larger in size than it ever was, simply because we were never prepared to face up to it properly.

Similarly, we often avoid taking a systematic approach to our problems. We say:

"A systematic approach to this problem would be painful and difficult, since I would discover my ignorance, weaknesses and limitations. Best, then, to avoid the whole business and, to avoid it successfully, I must avoid that I'm avoiding it!"

In particular, we will avoid making long-term and/or short-term goals. Both are necessary, of course; there is no use in having a vision of the horizon you would like to travel towards if you have no idea about how and where you will take the first few steps. Equally, there is little benefit in being a stickler for detail if you have lost sight of your longer-term goals and the overall context of meaning and purpose in which you are operating. Some of us can lose sight of the wood because we are so closely enmeshed in the undergrowth, while others make vast generalisations about woods while ignoring the fact that each of these does in fact consist of individual trees.

These are very common errors, and it is worth looking at why they are so commonly made. The 'stickler for (minute) detail' tends to get stuck at this level of activity, and loses an overall perspective, because he has discovered the value of looking at the short-term picture but is still rather scared of, or unaware of, the longer view. We tend to spend rather too much time practising the skills we are already good at, and not enough time in dealing with our weaker areas.

And so; some make a virtue out of looking at 'the fine print' yet fail to have a broader view, while others stay with their grandiose visions, while avoiding the actual details! The 'grand strategist' or 'ivory tower' theorist avoids examining the humdrum and short term intricacies, since he tends to feel rather insecure about these. To face them involves facing the realities of compromise and limitation, and these, for the theorist, are so much less imposing and reassuring than the grand vision that he carries around in his head.

27. I could deal with this problem more effectivelyif I would **write** things down.

Here is a commonsense suggestion that seems too obvious to mention except that so many people would benefit if they only tried it out. The very act of writing down our thoughts helps us to be more clear about just what these various thoughts are, and assists us generally to take a clearer and more systematic approach.

Frequently, we avoid this because we are scared that we will discover that we are hopelessly muddled, confused and at odds with ourselves about the problem. Facing up to such confusion can be painful and difficult (but not as difficult as *not* facing up to it!). The trouble arises because we so commonly take the view that we *shouldn't* be divided in ourselves, and shouldn't have contradictory opinions about the same thing. As a result, we are in the habit of pretending to ourselves and others that we are more clear and consistent than we really are.

Writing down all our contrary and contradictory views would, 'blow the gaffe' on our pretences to consistency and clarity; but it would help us to be more clear about what we are doing!

There is nothing to apologise about if we find that we are not 'of one mind' about a particular problem. It is, after all, only a *pretence* on everyone's part that we are consistent about what we think and feel. The normal reality is quite different, and we would be wiser, and less exhausted and uneasy with our pretence, if we were to face up to this! (See also section fifty-six, on 'internal conflict'.)

28. My trouble is that I am 'over-confident' but rather lacking in the competence needed to deal effectively with the problem.

Popular psychology makes a great play, these days, about the importance of confidence; and rightly so, because it is an important ingredient in success. If you don't expect very much from yourself or others, then you are likely to get as little as you expect. Moreover, with little confidence in your ability to do something you will tend to avoid putting yourself heart and soul into what you are doing. Consequently, you will have little chance of improving on your real competence and in discovering just what you are actually capable of.

Confidence, alone, though, is not sufficient. You do also need to learn to be *competent*; and 'confidence' can turn into a delusion of grandeur if we believe that we are really good at something when the plain truth is that we are not!

Some are confident, dogmatic, active – and *wrong*! Others are aware of the complexities, but paralyse themselves with their knowledge.

The trick, if you like, is to be 'half sure but whole hearted'; where we are prepared to really commit ourselves enthusiastically and confidently to what we are doing, without pretending that we are more certain and capable than is really the case. Confidence, then, becomes a trust in ourselves to cope as well as we can reasonably expect, without any illusions that events will always necessarily go our way, or that we will always do well, or that we have all the competence and skill that we would like.

If we are to be realistic, we would be wise to recognise that we will not often even manage to do our very best! After all, by definition, we spend most of our time doing only 'averagely well' in relation to our usual performance and capability. If we can accept this, we will find that we can be far more at peace with ourselves and our world and, paradoxically, we will discover that, by adopting this realistic attitude, we have a better chance of making the (realistic) best of ourselves!

It is an underlying *lack* of conficence that demands that we can, and should, always do our best; and that this 'best' will always be very good! Such overly optimistic and idealistic beliefs and expectations have little basis in reality, and effectiveness requires good 'reality-contact', however much it may conflict with our cherished hopes and ideals!

With *genuine* confidence and trust, we can face ourselves, our strengths and our limitations, as they really are and not as we would prefer them to be. It is only an appearance of confidence that denies all weaknesses and limitations, and pretends that all things are possible merely by the 'power of thought'. Charlatan claims like these, moreover, give popular psychology a bad name! (For example, book titles like *Think and Grow Rich* and *Grow Rich While You Sleep* might help their authors to become rich, but their implicit promise of 'riches' through positive thoughts and confident attitudes alone ought to be seen as self-evidently absurd. It is a sad commentary on the poor reality-contact of so many people that such titles can in fact make a fortune for the writer.)

It is useless if we so lack confidence that we undermine ourselves and underestimate our strengths. Such hesitancy prevents us from using our powers to the full. On the other hand, a lack of confidence serves a useful purpose if it warns us that our powers, knowledge and skills *are* limited, and that we are in imminent danger of over-reaching ourselves. Such hesitancy and caution does not hold us back; on the contrary, it helps us to use our full potential, by warning us to slow down and take a more careful, tentative yet more effective approach!

Undoubtedly, we can be too hesitant, and it can take some confidence to overcome this. However, there may be times when we are not hesitant enough. Confidence is required to deal with our hesitancy . . . and our recklessness! Caution and hesitancy, like many other qualities, can come in useful and useless varieties.

Too many – seemingly super-confident – people, who barge into a situation prematurely and brashly, do so because they are not confident enough to face their ignorance. If they were more confident, they would pause, hesitate, take stock, and come to terms with their limitations.

This culture readily recognises the kind of confidence that doesn't hesitate, and which 'jumps in and does'. It is not, however, very good at seeing the importance of the confidence that takes a quieter, slower more reflective and tentative approach. Sometimes we need to acknowledge that: "I have no right to feel very confident about this problem. After all, I am essentially *incompetent* with it at present." (See also section nineteen, on Confidence.)

29. I don't distinguish between an **urgent** problem and an **important** one.

Mostly, our lives are filled with urgent trivia. Our time, we believe, runs; and we consider that we must run too in order to keep up with it. And so every day consists of all kinds of relatively small matters that 'must' be done by a certain deadline. We 'must' get the children to school on time, get ourselves to work on time, get the meal ready on time, keep our appointments with others on time, get the shopping before the shops close, make sure that this particular project is fixed by the agreed date – and so on.

Now, I am not suggesting that we should simply ignore the clock and forget about keeping agreements and being punctual. It may be that we in the West are rather too obsessed about time but there is, nonetheless, something to be said in favour of tackling a task when we said that we would do it; and it would be impossible for us to make complex arrangements with others unless everyone was prepared to keep to an agreed timetable!

The problem is not that we are faced with urgent demands; this is probably inevitable in the kind of society we choose to live in, and there is nothing *necessarily* wrong with it. The problem, rather, is the way we tackle these urgent matters. Too often we let ourselves get overly tense and worried about them (see, also, sections 14, 36, 37, 55, 56, 61 and 68) and we let ourselves get buried in the urgent day-to-day issues so that we lose a proper sense of perspective on the role that these have, and should have, in our lives as a whole.

It is easy to get so lost in all the urgency that we forget that most of these very urgent matters are not really very important and, indeed, in the majority of cases we will, *even by tomorrow*, have forgotten all about those tasks that are presently so consuming and overwhelming us! We chase around madly with some presently urgent trivia, and completely fail to see that tomorrow we will be equally obsessively chasing after something else, while this present all-consuming crisis will have passed into history never to be thought of again!

It really is important to remember that a problem can quite

often be *urgent* without being very important, and, conversely, many of our most important problems are not particularly urgent! For example, it may be important that I examine some difficulties that I am having with spouse, children, or other relations, colleagues and friends. It may be useful for me to take stock of what I am wanting to achieve at work, or in my leisure time, or in the next 'stage' of my life. Or I may want to reconsider some of my more deep-seated methods, values, aims, ideals and beliefs. There are countless possibilities.

Yet none of these things need to be done 'by six o'clock tonight', or 'by the end of the month', or, even, 'by the end of the year'. It is all too easy, then, to keep on putting off these important longer-term problems and let ourselves be swamped by the more immediate, short-term trivia which, although they are each small matters of no long-term importance, all need to be completed by a fixed deadline.

Very tempting it is, to spend all our time with urgent trivia; particularly when we sense that the less urgent, more important, matters are going to be tricky to sort out, and will leave us feeling confused, uncertain and in conflict with ourselves. Generally speaking, the really important questions do not have neat, clear-cut and easy answers. Instead, they are vague and messy in shape. If we are to cope with them, we have to be tolerant of a good deal of doubt, compromise, and limitation.

Thus the attraction of getting back to the urgent day-to-day stuff which has definite and neat endings. With these, you can forget about the last problem and go on to the next, with all the added drama in asking "Will I, or won't I, get it done on time?"

In the short run, this short term approach works well enough, but we lose a longer-range perspective on what we are doing. Slowly but surely, the deeper-seated, but less urgent, problems build up on us.

Have you noticed how frequently people wait until a problem has become urgent before they get round to tackling it? For example, I will examine my relationship with my son only after he has become a delinquent; or I will consider the state of my marriage after my wife had threatened to sue for divorce; or I will start to worry about my social life and leisure time interests after I've discovered that I haven't got any; or I will examine my approach to work after I've been threatened with bankruptcy or dismissal; or, I will re-examine my attitudes to life and my behaviour after I have had a nervous breakdown!

Virtually everyone will be prepared to tackle a problem once it has become as urgent as all this. However, after ignoring a problem for this long, you will often find that matters have become far, far worse than they were in the beginning. It will be much harder to get on top of the problem, and you may well find that in many respects it is already too late to repair the damage that has been done by your neglect!

So often, people fear that if they try to tackle a major problem, they will only make a catastrophic failure of it; and they ignore it for so long that, in the end, it really *does* turn into a catastrophe! Then, they say to themselves, "You see, I knew that this would end up as a disaster. I did well to ignore it, because at least that delayed the evil day for a bit!"

The moral, surely, is clear. If a problem really is important, do try to deal with it before it becomes urgent and all the more difficult to solve. This will involve putting aside some of the less important, but more immediately urgent problems.

There is, of course, a third category of problems; those that are, right from the start, both important *and* urgent. For example, if one of your family is badly injured in an accident, it is both important and urgent that you get him to hospital as soon as possible. Problems like these can be very harrowing, and those with a disposition to worry uselessly will often entertain fantasies of how *terrible* it would be if something dreadful like this were to happen.

However, this kind of problem arouses no internal conflict, uncertainty and doubt. Its obvious urgency and importance leave us with no hesitation at all about whether or not we should tackle it. We just get down to it straight away as best we can. We have plenty of motivation even if the problem itself is very complex. When matters are really very urgent, we don't even have much time to be scared, un-confident or doubtful. We just get to it as best we can without a second thought.

When we imagine some crisis or another, we can become very fearful just at the *thought* of it. Yet when a crisis actually occurs people often discover that, to their surprise, they are not scared after all! They are too busy to be afraid, or too busy to have time to make the fear worse by thinking about how afraid they are! In these respects such 'difficult' problems can seem quite 'easy' to deal with!

Compare this with the final category of problem; the unimportant and non-urgent one. For example, sewing a button on a coat you wear only occasionally; cleaning a cupboard you rarely use; staying in contact with someone you only marginally want to see; sorting out some minor documents; putting your photos in an album.

These trivia, that are not even urgent, can often require a good deal of self-discipline if we are ever to tackle them at all. Whenever we think about them, we immediately find all sorts of other tasks which 'perhaps' we would be better off doing. We feel lethargic about them unless, for some personal reason, we will particularly enjoy doing them. We often feel bored and jaded at the prospect of doing them. We ask, "Shouldn't my life be more important than this? Is this all that I've got to do in my life?"

And so this non-challenging, unimportant, non-urgent stuff is often very difficult for us to tackle; even when the problem itself is intrinsically *simple*!

Such chores invoke a good deal of internal conflict within us. Whenever we get around to dealing with them, there is likely to be a large 'part' of us that is, as it were, saying: "I don't want to do this. This is a bore. I feel heavy, tired and exhausted. This is not worth doing at all!"

It is often very difficult to do something which we have 'just about' and 'on balance' decided to do. It is much easier, really, to do something when we are quite overwhelmingly clear that we want, or need, to do it. Because then, however difficult the task may be, we are at least in no doubt that we should/need/want to be doing it, and so it scarcely seems as though a decision was involved at all.

30. I am trying to do **too many** things at once.

Picture the following situation, and then consider how common it is and how often you yourself fall into the trap described: You have, say, half a dozen to a dozen different jobs to deal with, and let's assume that each is fairly urgent. What do you do? Well, if one job clearly needs to be done first then the decision is easy. But what if there is no particular order of priority or urgency? (And, remember, this is a very common situation for most of us!)

What frequently happens is that a person starts to tackle one problem and, straightaway, begins to ask himself, "Perhaps I should be doing one of those other jobs?" Then, having made virtually no progress on the first task, he switches his attention, and begins to fiddle with another problem. As time begins to run out, and all the problems become that much more urgent, he gets more and more restless, uncertain, and tense; and he scrambles away very briefly with each of the problems, moving impatiently from one to the other and spending only very short amounts of uninterrupted time on anything.

He says to himself, as it were, "I can't spend too long here because there are all those other problems that I have got to deal with soon. Unless I get back to them very quickly, they are likely to get completely out of hand". And so the person finds himself rushing around, and he does little more than survey all the various problems he has. Very little gets done, and as he realises this, and continually reminds himself of all the different things he has to do, this unfortunate individual gets more and more into a panic... which leads him to decide that he must rush all the more frenetically. A vicious cycle has developed.

Such a situation can be genuinely difficult to deal with because, sometimes, we really *do* need to switch from one job to the next before we have completed any of them. In other words, we need to do a bit of one, then a bit of another, then another, and so on. Women working at home with chores and children probably know more about this than most men; and they know, too, how demanding and exhausting it can be.

It is not so much that we are *literally* doing, say, ten jobs at once. If we are working well, we flow from part of one task to part of another to part of the next, and so on. This requires constant decision-making, assessment, re-assessment and awareness of what is going on outside of our immediate focus of attention. It becomes impossible to restrict our attention for very long to the job immediately before us because, in order to re-assess all the other jobs, we need to be switching our attention to the others, and briefly surveying them all, quite frequently.

All this requires considerable skill and, sadly, it tends to be a skill that is not very widely recognised and appreciated; probably for two reasons. Firstly, because this situation tends to be more of a woman's predicament than a man's; and women's roles, generally, still have less status than men's. Secondly, because the actual jobs that the person is switching between are not necessarily in themselves, and individually, very complex or difficult. And so we tend to ask "How can I be getting into such a state about such trivial things?"

The really difficult feature of all this is knowing *when* to make the switch from one job to the next, and, often, we fail to see that a difficult decision-making skill is involved, and so we underestimate the overall difficulty of what we are doing. This means that we can end up with a much lower opinion of ourselves than we actually deserve. We consider that, in these seemingly easy circumstances, we ought to be doing much better; whereas it may be that, in these actually quite difficult and challenging circumstances, we are doing quite well, or, at least, much better than we thought.

The work of 'experts' has much higher status than menial day-to-day domestic and child caring responsibilities. Yet computer scientists are in fact finding it much easier to write 'expert system' programs (that produce 'robot' versions of doctors or lawyers) than models of 'child care and household tasks'. The professional is likely to be replaced by a machine more quickly than the household manager who has a complex multi-task role that is beyond the skills of computer programmers to model.

Sometimes it can be very difficult to know whether we are just fidgeting with too many different problems at once, or making a reasonable attempt to keep abreast of them all. However, with the wisdom of hindsight, there is all the difference in the world between the person who is staggering, or 'skittering', ineffectually from one problem to the next, and the other person who moves with grace, and seemingly without effort, from one small piece of work to another.

A classic example of this skill in action, that most people are familiar with, is cooking. If you take many of the single elements of this job, they seem boringly easy; absolute child's play! Anyone can boil potatoes, cut up vegetables, put meat into an oven (though it takes some skill to peel and carve etc.). The real challenge, though, is to synchronise all these different tasks so that they are all completed at more or less the same time!

Of course, the cordon bleu chef takes such skills of synchronisation, along with other abilities, to sublime and exceptional heights. Nonetheless, I suspect that at least as much skill is required in cooking a more ordinary meal *and at the same time keeping three young children amused*!

So what can *you* do to improve your performance in this kind of situation? *Step one*, find out into which category you fit: Are you uselessly dithering and dashing about? In which case, trust that the other problems can be safely left for a while (set yourself an actual time limit!) and then focus your attention on the problem in hand.

Don't keep on saying to yourself that you could just as easily be doing one of the other jobs. That may very well be true, but so what? You can't literally do a dozen things at once, and, if there really is nothing to choose between priorities, then spin a coin! (Why not?) There is nothing necessarily 'wrong' with you or your circumstances if you find that the priorities you set yourself are fairly arbitrary. That is just the way it is sometimes; and why shouldn't it be like that?

On the other hand, maybe you discover that you really are faced with a variety of different challenges, and you do need to keep a fairly regular eye on all of them and move briskly and frequently from one to another. If this is so, then remind yourself that this is a major challenge for anyone. You can reassure yourself, and build up your confidence and morale, if you remember that many people with much higher status than you, who seem so much more successful, could not manage this challenge as well as you!

I am quite serious. Don't forget that most 'super-executives' and 'super-successful' career women have secretaries, research teams, advisers, nannies, cooks and cleaners. And so, although they may be facing a big challenge, with lots at stake, they are usually free to contemplate it without the constant interruption of other problems demanding attention. If this is not so then they are probably badly organised; since it really is most unwise to try to make important and significant decisions while you have many other (avoidable) matters buzzing around you at the same time.

Another point: People who are faced with low status, 'humdrum', but genuinely difficult problems, can have a tendency to feel inadequate, inferior and un-confident in relation to the celebrities and super-stars who have those more glamorous, exciting and 'important' challenges to deal with. Just remember, though, that in many ways it is much *easier* to be faced with an exciting, attention-getting, ego-enhancing problem than to have one of the more lowly, common-or-garden, sort! After all, the glamorous challenges provide people with so many obvious rewards of power, status, money, celebrity, attention etc.

Our more ordinary problems are, relatively speaking, thankless tasks, that consequently *deserve* more praise, even if they don't actually get it! This is worth remembering, because, even if others are not noticing what you are doing and giving you some sort of praise and recognition, you might at least start to give it to yourself and take a rest from moaning at yourself for only having these more lowly, everyday problems!

31. I am too much of a **perfectionist**.

We all, naturally, like to be able to do our very best when we approach a problem, and we would like our 'very best' to be very good indeed! There's nothing wrong with having ideals; it would be a poor state of affairs if we didn't. But are you one of those people who expects to be able to do your best *all the time*? If so, have you noticed how much you suffer needlessly as a result of this unreasonable expectation? By definition, you will most of the time only manage to put in your average performance; and for half the time you will be below your average. (This, after all, is the result of what is meant by an 'average'!)

It is foolish and self-defeating to make such a big fuss, as so many people do, when they are not operating at their best. We can *regret* it when we don't do so well as we might have done, and we can try to do better and learn from our mistakes. But why make a catastrophe of it? Have you noticed how, by 'catastrophising', you can make yourself unnecessarily miserable? Have you discovered that you get so tense and worked up about your performance that it actually deteriorates still further? Do you realise that by getting too upset about your mistakes, you fail to learn from them, and so you make even more mistakes?

It is quite unrealistic to imagine that even our best will always (or often!) compare well with others. We all find it easy to work away at a problem when we know that we are much better at it than almost anyone else. The real challenge is to plug away at something even though you know that you are just an ordinary (or perhaps rather a backward) performer. Nothing much would get done in this world if everything was left to the star performers. There simply aren't very many of these to go round!

Perhaps you are the sort of person who says, as it were; "I'm not going to get fully involved yet in this problem, because I'm not good enough; I'd only make mistakes". Or, "I'm not going to commit myself fully to these people around me; they don't deserve it, they're not good enough, they're not appreciative enough, or sensitive, or intelligent, or perceptive, or energetic, or wise enough. And so I'll wait until I find a better class of person/the 'ideal' partner."?

Do you have tendency to say, "I'm not going to really put myself into this problem yet because the whole set-up is wrong, inadequate, far from ideal. I won't tackle it yet; instead I shall wait until I'm fully informed, absolutely clear, properly prepared, and then the problem can be approached on exactly the right ground and in the right, just and fair set of circumstances. Then, I'll really get going, and I'll really show everyone what I'm capable of doing"?

There are of course times when it *is* wise to hold back and wait for a better set of circumstances, get yourself better prepared, and wait for others to make a few changes. But all too often people take this strategy to absurd lengths. We can so easily become perfectionistic, and this character-trait is to be found not just among idealistic and energetic youngsters, but also with the jaded, burnt out, cynical, and exhausted older person, who takes the view that everything is hopeless and that nothing significant can be done.

The disillusioned, burned out, individual has usually got into this position precisely because he has not been sufficiently willing to make compromises with reality at the expense of his fine plans and ideals. If we are to live at all, we have to live with, and in, the (imperfect) world as it is, and not with our dreams and fantasies of how it 'ought' to be. Otherwise we are not really living, but merely dreaming our lives away.

Some people drift towards the view that the whole of our life is a 'rehearsal' for the 'Great Day' when we, others and the world as a whole will be finally sorted out. The curtain will then be able to go up on the great new show called 'Life as it *should* be lived'. Such fantasies are nonsensical of course, if only because everyone has a different plan about how the show should be run, and everyone wants to be the director! This is not a rehearsal for when our lives are really going to get started; this is the actual performance, and we do much better with our problems when we approach them with this, more realistic, attitude.

Images of an ideal solution to our problem are fine, as long as they *help* rather than hinder us in tackling the problem. But our ideal image of 'the solution' often becomes a hindrance because, when we compare it with the outcome we are more likely to achieve, we allow ourselves to become disillusioned, demoralised and despairing and – not to put too fine a point on it – we *sulk*.

We would all prefer to be able to make our dreams come true, and to come up with entirely satisfactory answers to our problems. But, let's face it, compromise and limitation usually lie at the heart of everything we do, and we would be wiser (*and more effective*) if we were to come to terms with this.

Otherwise, (have you noticed?) we may find that, because we refused to make do with second or third best, we end up with *tenth* best, or nothing at all. Some take the view that "If I can't have it the way I want it, then I'd rather have nothing." But this purist and uncompromising approach is not heroic bravery against the odds; it is a stubborn stupidity that will not come to terms with

the imperfection and limitation that is an inevitable part of the
Human Condition. Such refusal to come to grips with actual
reality is not a courageous stand. It is simple cowardice.

You would need no courage at all if you really were as perfect,
all-powerful and all-knowing as you would like to be. But it takes
a good deal of courage to live our lives and live with ourselves
when we face up to and accept just how weak and ignorant we
are.

With a more positive approach to your problems you can avoid
feeling 'terrible' when events don't go to plan. You can simply
assume that, more often than not, the outcome will *not* go your
way. And then, on those rare occasions when all goes as planned,
you can look upon this as a wonderful, lucky, and rare bonus.
Don't expect your good luck to last though; then you won't be
surprised and disappointed when, surely enough, your luck runs
out!

We would never learn very much, or grow up very much, if
everything always did fit in with our plans. We learn the most,
about ourselves and the world around us, when Fate throws us a
few surprises. Some people suffer, and are weakened, because
'Fate' has been very harsh with them. Such victims of
circumstance need great reserves of courage and wisdom if they
are to survive. Others, though, suffer (in less obvious ways) and
are weakened because they have been coddled for too long in a
protected nursery where no chill winds ever blew!

32. I am looking for a **simple answer** to this problem.

Complexity is hard work! (Or, at least, it often seems like it). "If
only..." we say to ourselves, "... if only I could find a simple
answer that somehow or another got to the bottom of all this
complicated detail, and made everything lie down quietly." And,
sometimes, of course, there *are* simple answers; just often

enough, perhaps, for us to believe that there might *always* be a simple solution.

When a simple explanation is just as thorough, comprehensive and effective as the others, then of course we will prefer it. And some of our best and most profound explanatory theories do have a quite uncanny elegance and simplicity.

Sometimes, though, we are saddled with complexity and confusion; and even when this is a result of our ignorance we may still have to put up with it. It would be better for us if we could do this with good grace.

The alternative is that people will chase after, and, worse yet, pretend that they have got, a simple all-embracing explanation, when all that they have got is a simplistic, childish fantasy of an answer that is an escape from, rather than an explanation of, 'Reality'. Such escapism, sadly, is quite common.

When we are on the track of a real breakthrough in relation to our problem it is easy to work away at it, because we are getting such large rewards. No wonder, then, that we are tempted to imagine that we have 'seen the light' when we haven't! The real challenge is to keep at it when there is no such sign of a simple breakthrough, and when it feels as though we are churning around in the mud. 'Great leaps forward' occur only very occasionally – that is why we tend to get so excited about them. If they occurred all the time we would be quite blasé about them. It is easy to feel joyful and elated when everything is going our way; the real challenge is to see if we can find (a different kind of) peace and tranquility when things are *not* going so smoothly.

33. I am suffering from 'tunnel vision'.

Do you know the experience of having a 'method', or 'system', that really 'works'? Just for once, maybe, you've found a way of tackling a problem that brings dividends. No doubt you were very pleased with your discovery, and doubtless you made sure that you learned it well. No doubt, too, you went ahead and applied this effective approach as often as you could. The more it worked, the more attached to it you became, and the more you tried to find new ways of applying this method. Before long, a brand new and successful method would have been turned into a familiar, and somewhat over-used habit.

It is easy to slip into habitual ways of approaching problems, and, let's remember, we usually do this because, in the beginning at least, the approach we developed seemed to work quite well. If nothing else, it was better than anything else we managed to think of! Before too long we forgot to ask, "Is there a better way of going about this?" It becomes just too easy to go about matters in the way we have always approached them; and we settle down into a quiet, and comfortable rut.

Difficulties start to arise, needless to say, when we come across a problem which might, on the surface, seem like others we have tackled before, but which in fact is different in some crucial way or another. Maybe the circumstances surrounding the problem have changed, or other people's expectations of us are different or, even, our own abilities are not what they were!

In this kind of situation we then, so often, become (quite unnecessarily) stuck! It is not that we are unable to step back and take another approach. It is, rather, that we are unwilling to do so! We have made such an investment of time and energy in doing things in a particular way; this approach has generally worked in the past; and so we ask, "why, oh why, should I have to change now?" To do so seems like a terrible loss, and it feels just too painful and exhausting to have to 'go back to the beginning' and start again with the problem. It is regarded as an unwanted retreat rather than a valuable opportunity to try something new.

Even among the really 'expert' thinkers you find this tendency to stick too long with the old and familiar ways. In science, for example, you are supposed, in theory at least, to be entirely open-minded and ready to amend or abandon your tried and trusty hypothesis or formula, in the face of new evidence. You are then expected to look around and be perfectly willing to adopt a new theory if it explains both the new and the old data and, generally, gives a better account than your own theory (which you may have taken years to develop!).

So much for the ideal. In actual fact, scientists (like any other human beings) tend to hang on to *their* theories, procedures, beliefs, metaphors and explanations, even when the evidence has for some time strongly suggested that they should move on and try something new.

Worst of all, is when we start to think that the approach we are taking is a part of us. We can become as reluctant to lose such treasured ideas and methods as we would be to lose an arm or a leg! In other words, we can start to believe that this approach we are taking is in some way a part of our 'identity', and it can then become very difficult indeed for us to let go and try something new.

When the approach we are taking really turns out to be a hopeless flop in some new situation, that is evident for all to see, then we probably will, finally, after much pain and heart-searching, retreat a little and try another approach. Much more common, no doubt, are those occasions when we get by (just about) with our tired old ways of tackling things, and so never feel the need to take a new approach. In this way we will often fail to discover some different means of dealing with the problem which could have been far more effective if we did but notice it. And so we carry on indefinitely with a method which is substantially more inefficient, wasteful, unproductive and inadequate than necessary. Just how often this sort of thing may be going on we can have no way of knowing!

34. I simply **cannot solve** this problem and I need to accept that.

O.K., so you sometimes give up too easily. You say that you can't do something when in fact you *won't*; usually because of fear or a preference for an easier challenge!

We very rarely use our powers and potential to the full. When we say to ourselves or others that we are 'fully stretched', it is more likely that we are really operating with only one tenth of our energy, attention and commitment.

But do you sometimes go to the other extreme and imagine that there are no limits to what you can achieve? Do you imagine that, if you use your powers to the full, you can overcome every obstacle, deal with every difficulty and solve every problem? Do you believe that courage, persistence and determination will get you out of *every* difficulty? If you do, you are not taking a heroic approach to dealing with your problems; you are suffering from delusions of grandeur. Real courage recognises that there *are* limits to what is possible.

You may not be trying hard enough, or you may be trying too hard. The solution to a problem may come to you if you just leave it for a while. But, let's not deny it, sometimes that answer simply doesn't come at all! In which case you need to be at peace with this and give up the fantasy that you can always find answers to every question. What's more, there is no handy formula that will tell you whether you should be trying harder, trying less hard, or giving up altogether! Quite often it will be the case that we "don't know" and, moreover, "we don't know *why* we don't know"!

35. I need more of a **sense of humour**.

Humour comes in various guises, and it is the underlying spirit with which a joke is being made that makes all the difference. Some forms of humour are genuinely releasing and helpful for ourselves and other people. Other varieties, however, are highly destructive both to the 'humorous' individual concerned and to others.

For example there is a distinction, well worth making, between laughing with someone else and laughing at them. When we laugh *with* other people then that may be a really valuable release for us all. It helps us to stop taking ourselves too seriously; gets us out of the entrenched position we may have been stuck in, and gives us more of an overall perspective on ourselves and our problem.

When, on the other hand, we laugh *at* someone else, our humour can all too often be at the expense of the other person, without showing any compassion, toleration and respect for that person and his difficulties.

It is possible to laugh at another's folly and error in a humane way that is designed to 'pull them down a peg or two' without vindictiveness or violence. Usually, if the joking is of this more constructive sort, there will be some attempt to get the 'victim' to see the funny side as well; to include her rather than just use her as a target. The humour can really be shared when all concerned recognise that their own behaviour is as much of a joke as anybody else's!

We may do well to cackle when the 'puffed-up' and posturing individual slips on some banana skin. But let us remember that none of us is immune from such ego-centred folly. If we look down too much upon the stupidity of others (however stupid they may really be), we will hurt our victim with the underlying aggression and contempt that is involved; and damage ourselves with our hostile feelings and our delusory belief that we are 'above' others.

Humour, then, can be very releasing for us all, and can help us to breath again and let go of some of our tensions and pre-occupations. But it does also take some very destructive forms.

Another dangerous variety worth noticing is the hysterical or manic kind of humour that hides a variety of underlying feelings, like despair, fear, nervousness or rage. Humour can take our attention away from what is happening and from what is preoccupying us. But this is not always good for us. In some cases, we would be wiser to become more aware of the underlying feelings that have sparked off the hysterical laughter, and not keep on using humour as a means of escape. If you are frequently feeling despairing, or bitter, or afraid, or insecure, or angry, or tearful, then you might be wiser to face up to this, let the feelings out, and find out just why you feel this way. You then have a much better chance of coming to terms with the feelings, learning from them, and deciding what you are going to do as a result of what you have learned.

As ever, it is not possible to write a simple formula for all of this. And so, for example, some people who are always weeping, and feeling sorry for themselves would be better off if they could laugh sometimes at themselves and their predicament! But others would be of more service to themselves if they stopped their manic and hysterical laughter (at themselves or others) and had a good cry!

Even when we are directing the humour towards ourselves we may not necessarily be doing ourselves any good. It may be that the humour masks a contempt, aggression or despair towards ourselves and our own predicament; such that the humour is just a mask. It may amuse others, without being of long-term value to ourselves; hence the experience of some professional comedians who show a comic face to the public but who are chronically depressed inside.

Fortunately, we *can* usually tell whether the humour is 'healthy' or 'unhealthy' if we are genuinely prepared to be honest with ourselves. The really releasing sort of humour will leave us feeling more relaxed, closer to others, more aware and more tolerant and accepting of our faults and the weaknesses of other people. This kind of humour also leaves us feeling warmer towards ourselves and our fellow mortals. Our predicament may be as genuinely awful as ever, but with a joke we can show that our spirit is not defeated and that we can get what we can from life and come to terms with its limits. Consequently, we feel more at peace, we see more clearly, we are less swept away by our feelings, we have a new sense of perspective, we are renewed with new energies and a greater realism.

More destructive forms of humour change nothing. They merely postpone and exacerbate matters. Such humour might give us a temporary reprieve from negative feelings, but it doesn't actually get rid of them, and it doesn't help to be aware of these feelings and thus learn from them. And so we go on feeling haunted, tense, uneasy, despairing, confused, afraid, sad, furious, contemptuous, or whatever. The tension is there to be seen and felt (if we will allow ourselves to feel it) even as, and immediately after, we have finished laughing.

Think about the last time you laughed and ask, "Did I really feel better after that?" If the humour really did work for you then congratulations! You've just treated yourself to one of the best cures available for assorted human ills. However, if you did not feel (just slightly) better then either this was not 'good humour' or you are not presently taking a good humoured approach to it.

A supplementary question: Did you feel better because you saw your weaknesses and the failings of others with more toleration, peace and compassion? Or were you feeling better because, in your laughter, you felt more right, righteous, secure and justified in relation to others?

In other words, have you really come to terms with, and laughed about, human failings and limitation, or are your pride, pomposity and other hostile feelings merely masquerading in the form of a calm, quiet smugness and amused self-satisfaction? (Confession: I personally know a great deal about this trait in my own life. I think I am guilty of this kind of humour quite often; *and* of the hysterical, manic form which, for me, can mask an underlying sadness!)

Perhaps this can all be summed up in a nutshell: When you laugh, is there an underlying good-will towards both yourself and others? Or are you, beneath the smiles and humour, feeling an underlying *ill-will* and malevolence towards yourself, and/or others?

Face it, recognise it and learn from it if there is an underlying ill-will. Don't hide from it, or pretend that you feel 'peace, goodwill towards all' when you don't! Malevolence may well be destructive towards all concerned. It is particularly damaging to the person who is feeling malevolent. But it is even more destructive, and creates still further confusion and ignorance, to go around with a 'Polyanna'-smile and to pretend to feel what you don't feel!

It is bad enough when people feel hostile towards us and would seek to destroy us. But it is even worse when they pretend to themselves and us that they don't really mean us any harm, and would never feel anger towards anyone.

36. I need to stop **repressing** my feelings.

Do you have all kinds of negative, hostile and destructive feelings which you believe you 'shouldn't' have? And, have you noticed that, however much you may disapprove of these feelings, you often feel them all the same! What do you do about this?

Do you often feel guilty, 'bad', 'wrong', and inadequate for feeling the way you do? Do you punish yourself for having these dreadful/bad/wrong emotions and thoughts? (See also section twenty-five on *Guilt.*) Do you punish yourself with cruelty, malice and a lack of forgiveness? Do you consequently try to avoid feeling so badly about yourself by averting your attention away from these 'bad' and 'wrong' feelings? In other words, do you go unconscious-repress/avoid-remain unaware of your darker, murkier, more 'wicked' and generally unacceptable opinions, emotions, intentions, attitudes, and behaviour?

Such repression, of course, is tantamount to sweeping the matter under the carpet. And, as should be obvious, when you sweep mucky matter under the carpet, you don't actually get rid of it, or learn from it, or learn how to deal with it. You simply hide it from view; and – it builds up!

We hide away from ourselves all manner of unfinished business that we don't want to face; and so we tend to have a large accumulation of fermenting, rotting, 'festering', painful feelings and thoughts about many problems and issues that we have confronted (or failed to confront) in the past. They are painful to experience, and it is painful even to contemplate that we have them but might need to face them!

The danger here is that we can get ourselves into (yet another) vicious cycle: We fear that it is too much to face up to issues we have been running away from; and the more we run away from them the more threatening they seem. Moreover, the more such unfinished business piles up, the more we decide that there is just 'far too much of it' to deal with.

These repressed, unconscious thoughts and feelings don't go away, and they don't lie dormant either. Instead they influence our *conscious* feelings, thoughts and actions in many profound ways.

We don't notice how this is happening because we don't *want* to know; and we invent many rationalisations to explain what would otherwise be inexplicable behaviour. Anything, so long as we don't actually have to face up to the reality of some of these unacceptable and unconscious motives.

This leads us to become further and further out of touch with our *actual* motives, feelings, thoughts, fantasies and expectations; and, to this extent, we become that much less free, and that much more 'driven' as human beings. In other words, for as long as we are being influenced by unconscious thoughts, feelings, motives and intentions, we lack any real choice about them, and they rule our lives.

Frequently, some external stimulus will trigger off one or more of these buried feelings, and they will be, as it were, 're-activated'. We will fail to understand what is happening, since we will deny that the feelings are buried, and this will mean that we will have to invent some other story to explain what is going on. We will, generally, try to make ourselves 'right' and justified in our own eyes, and we will try to 'sell' to other people our own rationalisations. Often this will involve some blatent (or subtle) attempt to *blame* other people or circumstances for our behaviour. As we might guess, such avoidance, blaming and rationalisation can get extremely complicated, given that everyone else is likely to be engaging in the same kind of behaviour and thus seeking to collude with, make alliances with, isolate or blame others!

Human relationships are complex; but what often makes them

so much *more* complicated is our tendency to avoid, repress and rationalise so much of our experience and behaviour.

In the short run, this rationalising process will appear to give us some peace of mind; but at a more deep-seated level of experience we will often feel dimly uneasy and insecure. We will sense, however faintly, that we are in fact rationalising, repressing and avoiding certain issues which have led us to feel uncomfortable; and this discomfort can never be entirely removed by superficial 'cosmetic' cover-ups.

A room can never seem very clean and fresh if, over the years, people have always hidden the junk and rubbish away from immediate view; and, similarly, we will never feel relaxed, easy, clear and at peace for as long as we have been burying all manner of tension-making and painful experiences. It is all very well to duck an issue for a while, and this may even serve a useful purpose. (We cannot be expected to take on too much at a time.) But if we get into the habit of avoiding and repressing, and never, ever, face up to these buried away matters, then we will not give ourselves much peace in the longer term.

So, to repeat, what is to be *done* about this tendency to repress? There is a great deal that we can do: We can realise that avoiding a feeling does not change it, or deal with it; it just makes us less aware and thus less capable of handling it. However 'bad' or painful our experience may be there is always a great deal that we can learn from it; and we won't learn unless we face up to these negative aspects of life. Moreover, we will more easily be able to do this if we remind ourselves that we are not alone in having 'wicked', guilty secrets; everyone else has them too, however much they may put on a good show for us! And so we are nothing like as deviant as we may think. We are neither as good as we pretend nor as bad as we believe. We can reassure ourselves about this and take new heart from it.

Most important, we can try to make our voice of conscience a 'firm and supportive' friend rather than a 'harsh and domineering tyrant' (see section twenty-five), so that we will have less need to bury our feelings, and more of a capacity to forgive ourselves and others. In this way we can learn to control and discipline our thoughts and feelings (section sixty-five), with the realisation that genuine control and discipline does not arise from repression and self-hatred.

Understanding how all this works is not impossibly difficult; but putting this understanding into practice involves (as ever), trial and error, courage and... practice, practice, practice!

37. I need to stop **indulging** my feelings.

Indulgence is precisely the opposite of repression. Instead of thinking that our feelings are 'bad and wrong', we take the view that they are 'good and right'. And, instead of saying to ourselves that we 'shouldn't' feel this way, we say that we 'should' have these feelings, that we are bound to feel this way; that we are *made* to feel this way by all the 'bad' and 'wrong' people and circumstances who are the cause of our troubles.

Thus, far from hiding the feelings, we parade them to ourselves and others, and insist that we are bound to go on feeling like this indefinitely unless other people make the changes that they should and *must* make. Instead of feeling ashamed of our feelings, we feel *proud* of them.

This may seem, on the surface, to be a more desirable and more comfortable position to take than that of repression; and people, through pride, stubbornness, and self-righteousness, will cling on to such a state come what may. All too easily, we can pretend to ourselves that our own integrity is at stake (rather than pride and ego), and so we will defend ourselves to the utmost and refuse to give an inch. And all because, we say to ourselves, this is in our best interests.

But *is* such indulgence of feeling really in our best interests? Undoubtedly, it is not. Far from freeing us by taking an entrenched position, we imprison ourselves. We give ourselves no room for manoeuvre, and little opportunity to see what the matter looks like from a variety of perspectives. In this way, we fail to learn from other view-points.

Worse yet, we can make ourselves ill, miserable and chronically tense by endlessly 'cooking ourselves' in our own stew of wild and angry, painful, feelings. Indeed our own hostility and stubbornness almost always does more damage to ourselves than it does to anyone else (although it can be very painful for others too!).

When we indulge in anger and righteousness towards other people and to the world around us, we become less and less able to see what things look like in other people's eyes and less willing to forgive other people and come to terms with our own circumstances. We will thus take an increasingly jaundiced and depressive view of other people and the world as a whole, which will isolate us still further from others and from the support that we need from them. We will sink into the trap of taking a depressive view, which will lead us to withdraw still further. Such withdrawal will encourage us to be still more depressive, and so on, with depression and withdrawal feeding off each other indefinitely; unless and until we are prepared to break out of this trap.

The difficulty is that very few people, when they are indulging their feelings, are prepared to admit that this is what they are doing. On the contrary, they will say that there is no indulgence involved at all, and that they are merely asserting themselves, upholding their own honour and integrity, showing people 'where they're at', defending themselves against the attacks of others – and so on. And, if you attack this position, and try to show them that they are mistaken, they will be all the more likely to defend themselves and insist that they are right.

When people become self-righteously attached to a particular position, perspective, opinion or feeling, they can easily become *stuck* with it rather than supported by it. They start to stake their reputation, identity and integrity on maintaining this particular 'trench' come what may, and regardless of the cost to themselves and others. They take the view that, if they were to let go of their position even just a little, they would be losing ground, losing face, and completely 'at sea'. The matter then becomes a battle with 'winners' and 'losers'; where changing your mind, being open to other people and their views, being flexible and willing to compromise is seen as losing.

In this situation, any kind of attack on the position of another will be met with a strong defence; and the stronger the attack, the correspondingly stronger will be the defence, with all the propaganda, evasions, subterfuge, counterattack, dishonesty and deviousness that is involved in an actual military conflict.

If people are not ready or willing to let go of feelings and perspectives that they are clinging onto and indulging, then there is not a great deal that other people can do about it. And so you, the reader, if you are unwilling to examing any 'indulgences' that you may nurture, will, as you read this section, quite easily be able to say to yourself, "Oh yes, how true. I can think of several people who are like that. Of course, that is not one of *my* difficulties!"

Likewise, others accuse me at times of stubbornness and of refusing to budge. Of course, I know that they themselves are just being pig-headed and manipulative and trying to undermine my position. So I have to hang on and defend myself against them at all costs!

So often we take the view that a part of our very identity is at stake when people suggest that we might think or feel differently and change some of our more cherished attitudes and ways of behaving. We think to ourselves, "this is the kind of person that I am. If I were to let go of these particular thoughts and feelings, I would have become so different that I would hardly know who I was! Such a big change would be like death. And so I will resist it in every way I can."

If, though, we can start to see the price we are paying in being so rigid; in terms of our own misery, blind inability to see the views of others, and consequent isolation from them; then we may just start to be willing to be a little more ready to give and take, and to develop more of a perspective on our own feelings. We don't have to say either that these feelings are right or that they are wrong. They just 'are' what they are; and the wise move is to learn from such feelings and see how far they are of service to ourselves and others – without either repressing or indulging them.

None of this is easy, of course, and it is made more difficult by the fact that there *are* times when our integrity is at stake; where we should take a stand; should make sure others know how we feel, should maintain and assert our position. If there was *never* any virtue in making a stand then we would all easily be able to see through every ego-centred individual who was rationalising in this way. As it is, the matter is more difficult. As a rough guess, though, I would suggest that for every occasion where someone is 'standing in their own integrity' there are ten other instances where they are indulging their feelings. The difficulty lies in distinguishing between an honourable firmness and an indulgent stubborness and – you guessed it? – there is no simple, infallible, test that will make this distinction for us!

Nonetheless, it remains true that we are imprisoned within our positions rather than fortified by them. Our positions do not support us, they trap us. Locked within them, we no longer have much room to explore, to negotiate, to search for new solutions, to make compromises, and to look at the matter from the point of view of others.

Most important, when we are imprisoned within our position we fail to look at the underlying desires and needs that lie beneath this position. Moreover, the position of others gets in the way of our being able to see the underlying desires and needs that they may have. If we could manage to see these needs more clearly we could all the more easily find some compassion, understanding and respect – for ourselves *and* others.

38. I need to be more **flexible** and less rigid.

Do you tend to think that the 'strong' person is the one who takes a position and holds on to it come what may? Is the strong person firm, unyielding, rigid, indomitable and inflexible? Is he the one who doesn't give way, who stands like a rock, unmoving, regardless of whatever is thrown against him?

When you think of strength, do you tend to think in terms of images like cast iron and other such firm and unyielding objects? Do you consider that anything that has a bit of 'give' in it – like water, or a willow tree – is weaker, more 'wishy-washy' and generally less desirable?

In fact, the object (or person) who refuses to bend is far more likely to break. And so, for example, water has enormous power to find a way through and to resist the impact of other objects; a power that is not weakened by its capacity to give way to other forces.

Strength, then, does not have to be about defying and resisting the world around us; it has at least as much to do with being able to bend and accommodate to outside circumstances when these are too powerful to ignore; and to do this without cracking and breaking up altogether. This requires flexibility, an ability to come to terms with that which we can't change, and to work effectively with what *is*.

If we are really strong, we will have the courage to go after what we *can* achieve; but also the grace to accept that much will continue to lie beyond us and outside our range of ability. The strong person does not entertain delusions of grandeur, but knows that there are limits, and is at peace with this.

It is so easy to imagine that rigidity is a sign of strength, when in fact it is *flexibility* that is the sign of a really strong person. Having said this, though, it then becomes possible for genuinely weak individuals to try to rationalise their lack of decisiveness and courage by pretending that they are being flexible. For example, a person puts off ever making decisions, and pretends that this is because he is trying to be flexible about unforeseen circumstances that may arise. Or, perhaps, he is constantly changing his mind as soon as anyone puts the slightest pressure on him to do so, and pretends that this shows how flexible he is.

Clearly this is not flexibility. Such an individual is not taking a subtle, courageous yet sensitive, flexible approach. On the contrary, he is acting according to two simple, inflexible and unsatisfactory principles: ie. 1. "Avoid mistakes by avoiding decisions for as long as possible." 2. "Try to get approval from everyone by agreeing to whatever they want!"

39. I need to be more open-minded.

It is important to distinguish between having an *open* mind and having a vacant or *indecisive* mind. Take the person who is indecisive: Who won't stick to any decision she has made, but keeps on wavering and changing her mind under the slightest pressure. This isn't open-mindedness; rather, such a person allows him or herself, usually as a result of fear and a lack of confidence, to be blank or weak-minded, and may not be relied upon to come to a conclusion about anything.

Sometimes, such indecisiveness arises because the person is so aware of the complexities and subtleties of life; so sure that (s)he will never know as much as (s)he needs to know; and so reluctant to make a mistake. She fails to make any decision since she can so clearly see that it may be wrong; and, if she ever does decide anything, she easily changes her mind, since she has so little confidence in the decisions she actually has made.

There are (many) occasions when we need to decide and act even though we may well make a mistake; and we frequently have to choose on the basis of 'incomplete' information. After all, is there ever an occasion when we have all the information that may be useful?

We can rationalise our indecisiveness with the pretence that we have an 'open' mind; and some people react to this weak position, and imagine that, in order to be strong, we must go to the opposite extreme of being far too firm and decisive. This produces the kind of person who has definite and fixed views and never mind that the evidence is vague, inadequate or contradictory. Here, the mind is closed and prejudiced. The person has, literally, 'pre-judged' the answer to the problem and has a firm and final view when the evidence would indicate that he should be much more tentative, hestitant and open to new ideas and information.

It is often difficult to find a balance between being too fixed in one's views and too tentative. If we make judgements and draw conclusions prematurely, then we will not be making best use of the information that is available to us. But, equally, if we always refuse to make any pattern from the data before us then, once again, we will not be making proper use of our information and evidence. Real strength comes from being neither too fixed nor too tentative, but from finding a balance between these two extreme positions.

Most difficult of all is the ability to be both *tentative* about what we observe and believe to be true and *decisive* in our actions. If we are not tentative, then we will generally be pretending to know more than we really do know. And yet if we are not also decisive (in our actions) then we will not be using our powers to the full, and we are less likely to achieve anything if we never put ourselves into it heart and soul. In other words, we ideally need to be 'half-sure but whole-hearted'! This is a very difficult balance to achieve, but it is what we need to do if we are to find the best way of tackling a problem.

Some people find that it takes courage to make a decision, and they feel safe and more secure if they just keep on putting things off all the time. That way, they imagine, they will be less likely to make any mistakes. (Except that this whole strategy of procrastination is itself a big mistake.)

There are others who find it uncomfortable to put off making a decision and who prefer to rush into a conclusion and to take action long before they are really ready to do so, and before they have sufficient evidence for any conclusion or decision. For these people, it takes courage to leave things open and 'in the air' for a while. They would rather rush in and take almost any decision, however bad, in order to avoid the discomfort they feel when a problem is unresolved and undecided.

All this should indicate that you need to take an open mind about what it means to be 'open-minded' in any particular situation! The open mind is not blank, nor prejudiced, nor indecisive; it can be tentative in its perceptions while committed in its actions; and it will be open enough to know that it can't know in advance how long it can reasonably delay before drawing conclusions and taking action!

40. I need to be less angry and **irritable**.

Do you believe that we should never feel angry; that anger is always wrong and destructive; that we should always avoid it and always try to be peaceful, warm, loving, caring and sensitive? Such principles seem to me to be quite unrealistic. They demand far more of people than they can ever realistically be expected to achieve; and they also ignore the value and purpose of anger, and other strong, 'negative' emotions.

In certain circumstances anger is essential as a means of protecting ourselves against intrusion, invasion and exploitation by other people. Similarly, other people sometimes need to get angry as a means of protecting themselves against us! Thus anger has a value in defending ourselves and our integrity against what we judge to be morally unjust interference from others.

In this way, anger has at times served us well, and its biological roots can be seen in other mammals who, if they are not running away from a threat, will roar and rage in defiance against it, and use their anger as a way of summoning all their courage and strength to deal with a predator (or their evening meal!).

There is no doubt that some people would have more respect for themselves, and would gain more respect from others, if they allowed themselves to feel angry and to express this anger on occasions.

It is not necessarily catastrophic or even destructive to have someone show that they are angry with you. When someone gets angry with me, I might be wise to ask myself just what it could be that I am doing that is contributing to the other person feeling this way! In other words, anger can be a useful form of feedback. It is one of the ways in which we learn just how we are regarded by other people. Indeed, for some people, who are otherwise rather insensitive to the ways others react to them, anger is one of the few emotions which, because of its strength, they are actually able to detect. Any more subtle feelings can, on some rather thick-skinned folk, pass almost completely unnoticed!

However, there are many ways in which anger can lead us into difficulties, and become useless or positively destructive. For example, a person might repress her feelings of anger, because she considers that it is wrong to feel this way. (See section twenty-five.) The feeling then festers away under the surface of awareness, and is acted out in a variety of destructive ways of which we remain unconscious.

Or the person can become self-righteous about the anger (see section twenty-one), taking the view that she is absolutely 'right' to feel this way. She then indulges the feeling and concludes that she is bound to stay like this until the other, 'bad' and 'wrong' people or circumstances change their intolerable ways. Sadly such an individual tends to stay stuck with the feelings for a very long time, since few people are ready, willing or able to change very much just to suit someone else's principles or preferences.

Another way in which anger (or, for that matter, any other emotion) becomes destructive is when it is used as a weapon or a manipulative device. In other words, all too often we will not, simply and honestly, show our feelings in order that someone else knows how we feel; rather, we will use the feelings to undermine, or assault, or bully, or blackmail, or manoeuvre, or trap, or hypnotise another person so that he or she fits in with what we want. And, needless to say, others will do the same with us.

This helps to explain why interpersonal relationships are often so difficult to understand and keep track of. The difficulties arise because the parties concerned so often use dishonest means to get others to do what they want. And, because the means *are* dishonest, everyone will deny that they are doing any such thing. And so we are faced with layer upon layer of dishonesty, camouflage, propaganda, strategem, image-making, and 'conjuring tricks' of various sorts on the part of all concerned. In other words, getting to the root of people's motives, intentions, conflicts, expectations, underlying feelings and attitudes can be difficult enough at the best of times. But it is made ten times more difficult because, so often, people are not willing to be honest with others (or even themselves!) about what all these emotions and so on actually are.

What has all this got to do with problem-solving? A very great deal, given that few of our problems are dealt with in isolation from others, and the state of our interpersonal relations often has a very great influence on the way in which we co-operate, or *fail* to co-operate, in dealing with problems. Good reason, then, to try to see how, for example, anger is being used in a particular situation; and good reason to be uneasy when feelings are being buried or distorted. Often it will be difficult to get beneath the surface and see just what *is* going on because, even with a strong emotion like anger, it is only exceptionally that a person has a 'clear', clean and strong outburst of feeling.

Far more common are those messy, confusing and uncertain situations where you might have a vague suspicion that the other person is angry or irritated, but you are not altogether sure because the feelings are being expressed, or acted out, in mild, subtle and devious forms. It becomes hard to put your finger precisely on what is going on and to determine whether or not people are being manipulative. But what makes all this so much more difficult is the fact that manipulation, by its very nature, is a strategem that a person conceals very carefully beneath all manner of rationalisations, denials and distractions.

A crucial part of manipulation is the denial that the person is doing any such thing. And, while we are lamenting the way that other people go in for this 'terrible' behaviour, let us remind ourselves that we can rationalise and manipulate too, and let's see if we can set an example to others by facing up to it in ourselves!

To do so requires a substantial degree of genuine humility, honesty, courage and open-mindedness. We have to swallow a good deal of pride, be ready to forgive ourselves for a life-time habit of self-deception and rationalisation and, if all this wasn't enough, be ready to face up to the very real possibility that the 'opposing party' will use our openness and honesty as a way of trying to gain a tactical advantage over us in the manipulative contest that *they*, at least, have not abandoned. It is not surprising, then, to discover how difficult it is to give up all these games. Certainly, it is so much easier not to bother or, more cunningly, to pretend to be more honest and less devious, while using this pretence as yet another strategem for gaining an advantage over our adversary!

It is so much easier to begin hostilities than it is to bring them to an end, because by then we will have generally got ourselves into a vicious cycle of mistrust breeding mistrust breeding mistrust, which is very difficult to break. However, if we *can* achieve some increase in real good-will the benefits are enormous. Because we can then actually get on with tackling the problem with the genuine support and co-operation of others! No bad thing!

Perhaps the most destructive use of anger is where it is utilised as a weapon of revenge against another person, and is employed with the deliberate intention of hurting that person. This sort of thing occurs when we take the view that we have been unjustly, unfairly or meanly treated by someone else. We feel hurt by what they have done, or not done, and we take the 'eye-for-an-eye, tooth-for-a-tooth' approach to morality. In other words, we strike back at them.

The anger, in these circumstances, seethes beneath the surface and fuels a cold-blooded, systematic, devious, malicious and ruthless attempt to undermine and injure the other person. Usually this will involve a denial that any revenge is being sought, with perhaps a cunning cover-up of the 'dirty-work' that is being done! This kind of action can be more destructive of relationships than more overt expressions of emotion.

The worst outcome is where both sides in a dispute engage in the same pattern of revengeful behaviour, with each side covering-up its attempts to sabotage and injure the other party. Each camp, insofar as people are prepared to admit that there is a conflict at all, insists that 'God is on their side' and that *they*, and not the other people, are the blameless innocents.

The 'evil empire', needless to say, is always to be found among the bad people from the opposing camp and not among the angels and other fine folks who agree with us and are our friends! Truth becomes the first casualty in such warfare and a great deal of hurt can be inflicted. This is covered up and expressed as (still more) anger. Each side then becomes so entrenched in its position that it even comes to believe its own propaganda and fears that any giving way to the other side will undermine its own defences. And so any kind of empathy, toleration, mutual respect and compromise is, in such extreme cases, ruled out as weakness and treachery which might lead to the possibility of defeat.

Please don't imagine that this kind of entrenched and conflictual position is all that rare. I would suggest it is very common in all kinds of situations; at home, at work, and between groups, organisations and nations. Sometimes the conflict is very apparent and obvious for all to see. Just as often, though, the reality of the battle is hidden beneath the surface and left unstated and unexpressed. Instead it is 'acted out' in the behaviour of the conflicting people and groups and can be 'scented' through the poor co-operation, lack of trust, and the reluctance to share information and work together.

Sometimes people can be at loggerheads with each other, and can be making regular attempts to undermine and outmanoeuvre the other side, while all the time denying that they are doing any such thing. (For to do so would put them at a disadvantage in the conflict.) Indeed, there can be times when we are fundamentally at odds with others without really knowing that this is so and without consciously thinking about it at all. Not surprisingly, this is the hardest kind of conflict to try to deal with.

Another point about anger: People not infrequently take the view that anger (and other emotions too) just sweep over them, quite independently of their own will and judgement. And so, whereas most of us are prepared to take responsibility for what we *think*, you will often find that people will look upon their *feelings* in the way that they view the weather; ie. with the belief that it just comes and goes and changes quite outside our own control of it.

This view that emotions are outside of our own control, and that they exist and operate quite independently of our thoughts is a myth. And it is a very dangerous and destructive myth at that. How we feel does certainly colour and influence the way we think, but it is worth reminding ourselves that this process works in the opposite direction as well, such that what we *think* has a very strong impact on what we *feel*. Indeed, it is probably a mistake to talk of 'thinking' and 'feeling' modes of being as though each operated independently of the other. They are closely intertwined; each being both cause and effect of the other. They are in fact simply aspects of one overall personality, and they cannot be considered in isolation one from the other.

Whenever thoughts and feelings are separated off in this way you will find that the part that is ignored or denied has a very strong, but unrecognised, influence. For example, it is often the case that the thinking, rational, logical, dispassionate sort of person, who denies that he is in any way influenced by feelings, and will even deny that he *has* any feelings – will probably be dominated by a whole set of emotions that he is quite unaware of. So, for example, many of his very fine thoughts will in fact be the slaves of, and in service to, unacknowledged feelings.

Conversely, you will find that the emotional, romantic, intuitive, sensitive, feeling sort of person, who pays great attention to, and is greatly preoccupied with, the emotional side of her life, will in fact be dominated by a particular set of beliefs, judgements, opinons, attitudes, expectations, intentions – *thoughts*, that she is quite unaware of. It will be these various thoughts that will generally determine what the person is *feeling*.

Hence, for example, the intuitive person's feelings of anger, far from welling up spontaneously from some non-rational place 'in the heart', quite removed from the brain, will in fact be determined by a particular set of judgements, expectations and opinions about how people 'ought' to behave in specific circumstances; and by perceptions and interpretations of the intentions and behaviour of all concerned. The anger will arise, as it generally does, because reality has not lived up to the blue-prints and expectations of the person feeling this emotion.

Finally, let us remember that, on many occasions, when we would seem to be extremely angry with somebody else, we are mainly angry with *ourselves* for not being assertive enough. Our lack of assertiveness can infuriate us and, quite commonly, we will blame the other person for bringing our timidity to our attention. We then get all the more angry with them!

We will fail to deal with the underlying problem for as long as we are always blaming the other person and not coming to terms with what it is in ourselves that is annoying us.

Another version of this blaming takes place when we detect in someone else some quality that is also in ourselves and which we dislike intensely. Seeing it in others then sparks off the discomfort in ourselves; but, rather than be honest about what is happening, we once again restrict our attention to the failings of the other person in order to avoid looking at our own similar weaknesses. This gets us precisely nowhere. We rage at the other person, while feeling a growing unease in ourselves. An unease which we won't face up to and learn from. This can easily become another vicious cycle.

41. I need to be less **resentful** ...

Resentment can, of course, involve *anger*; it is possible, though, to be resentful without actually expressing, or feeling, much – or any – anger at all. Instead, the judgement that one has been injured and affronted leads to a duller, more sullen kind of feeling that is less dramatic than anger but more insidious in its effects.

As with all emotions, resentment can come in useful, less-useful, and useless varieties. It can serve us well when there really is a danger that we will be exploited, ignored, injured or invaded. The feeling of resentment can then assist us in standing up for ourselves and help us to push back the intrusion of others, so that our integrity and self-respect can be preserved.

However, our resentments may not be reasonable at all; but based upon unrealistic expectations and demands. In such cases we need to come to terms with the limitations that genuinely exist in other people and our circumstances, be less harsh in our judgements, and thus get rid of, or reduce, our resentment. This involves developing ideals that are a little more realistic and in line with what is actually possible instead of hankering too much after utopian fantasies. In other words, the 'ideal-ideal' is a 'realistic-ideal'! Demand too much and you will simply give up in despair.

It is not easy to judge whether it is we or others who are being overloaded; and difficult, too, to determine whether we are the aggressor or the victim! We may feel very confident about this yet still be wrong, either because we are habitually non-assertive, or bullying, or utopian or cynical. There are, after all, plenty of people who imagine that they have good cause to feel resentful of others, while these others are equally convinced that *they* are the injured party!

There is no simple, handy formula that will tell us how far our judgements and expectations are accurate and realistic, and no objective forum or individual that can infallibly determine any Final Truth about people's judgements and expectations. This is the sort of thing that can make life so frustrating and such fun! We have to trust our own judgements, in the final analysis, even though these, like everyone else's, are fallible and do not reliably give us the Last Word on anything. Trusting one's own judgement, mind, does *not* mean ignoring what others have to say, or pretending that we live as isolated individuals in a social and moral vacuum. It is surely wise to weigh very carefully the views and opinions of others, even though we ourselves inevitably have the last word when deciding whether or not, for example, this other person really *is* an authority who we would wish to follow.

We each, for ourselves, have the last word on a moral decision, but I hope it is clear that I am not thereby advocating a world of selfish pleasure-seeking or self-obsession. The buck stops with us when we make a moral choice; but our choice, I would argue, is a wrong one if it is made merely on the basis of self-obsession or a narrow self-interest. Moral judgements have to be made by individuals, each for themselves; but that does not make them purely and arbitrarily matters of individual opinion.

The lack of final certainty about judgements may seem a terrible thing to contemplate, but it can also be quite exhilarating. Just reminding ourselves of it can be a salutary and valuable experience that will help to prevent us from taking too tight a grip on our own position. Such an ability to avoid being too attached to our own 'objective' viewpoints may indeed be the nearest that we can ever get to any sort of objectivity. With a tentative open-mindedness it becomes possible for there to be real dialogue, mutual respect, empathy and compromise.

The problem, really, is not so much that people don't have a Rock-Solid Absolute from which to survey the world; I can't see that we are ever going to have this. The real problem, rather, is that so many people either think that they can't survive unless they get hold of some Final Certainty, or imagine that they have indeed got it all sorted out, when they haven't, can't and never will!

We never seem to be able to get the Final Word on anything, and although we often crave that we *could*, I suspect that we would find it terribly dull if we ever did! Nor does this have to mean that we become empty-headed, weak-willed, indecisive and unable to take an overall perspective and an independent opinion for ourselves.

When we feel resentful, then, as with all our other feelings, we need to reassess the underlying judgements and expectations that have fuelled this resentment; and we need to consider whether or not the judgements are accurate and the expectations realistic. It is not enough just to say "go with the feelings", "let it all hang out", "I feel it, so it's real and right". This can lead to a destructive indulgence of emotion that is of no help to anyone.

However, even if we do consider that the feelings are being fuelled by inaccurate judgements and unrealistic expectations, it does us no good to punish ourselves too harshly about this (see section twenty-five... on 'guilt'). We need to avoid both the repression and the indulgence of feeling.

Even if we consider that our judgements and expectations *are* 'right' and 'reasonable', we still might ask whether, for example, our resentment is serving any useful purpose. In other words we can ask of any 'complex' of thought and feeling (they are inextricably linked) – *Is it right? Is it reasonable?* and (even if the answer is 'yes') we can still ask: is it useful, is it effective, to go on and on with our resentment?

42. I need to be less **proud** and arrogant.

Pride can be a vice or a virtue depending on what sort of pride you have in mind. Let's first consider what might be called false pride:

It would seem obvious, unless we think more deeply about it, that the person who is (falsely) proud and arrogant must have a high opinion of himself. Surely he, of all people, considers that he is 'better' than others, smarter, more attractive, more successful, ... a 'winner'. The pride, we think, comes from our taking a lofty view of ourselves; and, conversely, the arrogance is a result of our looking down on the lowly inadequacy of others. In our arrogance we can take the view that these lesser mortals would do well to let us make all their decisions for them, were we ever to deign to do so.

In certain respects, the proud and arrogant person does take such lofty and condescending views, and he does indeed tend to have very grand ideas about who he is and what he is capable of.

However, it is worth pointing out that these grandiose ideas that the ego-maniac has about himself are just that – *ideas*! They will not have much basis in reality because no one has ever been remotely as wonderful, perfect, flawless, capable, and altogether 'right' as the proud and arrogant individual imagines himself to be! In other words, individual pride and arrogance is invariably based upon the *illusion* that we are more capable and coping than in fact is the case.

Such pride and arrogance makes us ineffective because it is based on illusions about our abilities, rather than an accurate and realistic assessment of what we are and are not capable of. Think about this, and it should be clear that illusions of any sort are a poor basis and recipe for effective problem-solving! All too often the proud individual will over-estimate his ability to deal with a problem, and will be reluctant to seek the help of others since he will consider that:

a. He doesn't need this help, and

b. Others are in any case unable to offer him anything given their own weaknesses and inadequacies.

Furthermore, he will avoid facing up to any of his own mistakes and weaknesses because this would threaten his precious image of himself and his capabilities. Consequently, he will tend to make a worse job of any problem than would otherwise be the case, though, of course, he will do all he can to avoid considering this.

Why do some of us become proud and arrogant? If it is based on illusion, rather than real evidence, why do we allow ourselves to be so easily deceived? The reason, surely, is that underneath all the posturing there are deeply seated feelings of insecurity, inadequacy and low self-esteem. (We have examined this to some extent in section nineteen, on *confidence*.)

The person who struts and postures, yet who hides away his weaknesses and limitations from himself and others must lack *genuine* pride and respect for himself. If he really did like himself, then he would be able to face up to himself as he really is, with all his (inevitable) conflicts, fears, doubts, weaknesses, failures and limitations. It takes enormous (real) pride in oneself to be able to look at oneself with honest humility. Only when we have an underlying *shame* about much of our behaviour and limitations do we feel this need to pretend to be better than we really are, and to strut around in front of others!

And so, another paradox, the person who is 'puffed up' and who seems too 'proud' before the world will be likely to be suffering from an underlying lack of trust, and a lack of (real) pride in himself. Whereas the person who can, with humility, come to terms with his limitations, will need enormous courage, respect and (real) pride in himself in order to be able to face this ordinary, limited, human being. It is easy to parade a false and inflated self before ourselves and others. It is much more difficult to face ourselves as we really are and let others see this as well, without feeling the need to hide away or to defend ourselves. *Anyone trying to deal with any kind of problem will be enormously fettered for as long as they are 'having to' live with illusions about themselves and their capabilities; and the truth, in most cases, is that we are neither as good as we pretend nor as bad as we believe.*

If you have good contact with reality, with what you can and can't do, and with what you are skilled and less skilled in doing, then your chances of making an effective job of a problem are much enhanced.

Another paradox: We hide away from ourselves and others what we consider to be the 'ugliness' in ourselves and our behaviour. But this produces an illusory self which is itself ugly! If, instead, we included all the 'bad' bits when we present ourselves to the world there could come from this an extraordinary beauty. People's attractiveness, in other words, comes not from a pretence at being more special and extraordinary than they really are, but from an honest and open revelation of themselves in all their ordinariness and limitation. This ordinariness, ugliness, limitation and insignificance then becomes quite extraordinarily beautiful, significant and heroic!

Such a theme has been explored in the arts from time immemorial, where we see how weakness hides behind a parade of strength and grandeur, while real strength and magnificence sits within ordinary mortal humans *because of* (rather than despite) all their failings and fragility.

It should be clear in all this that there is a place for a certain sort of pride (though not arrogance). When pride consists in a sense of satisfaction and well-being for what we really can do, and a basic liking of ourselves regardless of our limitations, then it is a very valuable, in fact essential, quality. Without a basic sense of self-respect and self-esteem it is very difficult indeed to live our lives with any peace or fulfillment. Only when we become proud of an *illusory* idea of ourselves does pride become destructive. But, as we have seen, this form of pride is perhaps really just an appearance that hides an underlying shame, low self-esteem and lack of genuine pride in ourselves.

Arrogance is always destructive of ourselves and others because it fails to recognise the positive qualities and potentialities of other people, and thus fails to draw these out. A person with real humility will be far more skilled in empowering other people and helping them to use their capabilities to the full; but this does not mean that he will hide his own strengths and skills, or pretend to be less capable than others when he is actually more skilled.

The arrogant person postures on the surface, yet is plagued with doubt underneath. He seeks to attract praise and applause yet, when he receives them on those occasions when they are genuinely earned, he has difficulty in accepting them. This is because this (deserved) praise clashes with his underlying feelings of self-doubt, self-deprecation and uncertainty! He claims to deserve praise when he really does not; yet when he both deserves and receives acclaim – he doesn't really know what to do with it! (Though sometimes he will seem to 'take it for granted' as a way of brushing it aside and thus – *avoiding* it!)

Some arrogance, then, is a mask. It hides from us the pain we would feel if we confronted the unused potential in ourselves and others. This pain exists because we would dearly like to see people actually using their potential rather than wasting it!

In other words, underneath the pain is a potential for love for others that we can scarcely bring ourselves to acknowledge! (And which we may be quite at a loss to know how to express.) Some might look upon others as 'scum' and 'animals', yet buried deep beneath such contemptuous attitudes there may well be a sadness at the waste of potential to be observed in all of us. We don't feel contempt for non-human animals since we do not consider that they (unlike us) are wasting their talents.

43. I need to be less **selfish**.

In industry and commerce these days great stress is laid on the importance of teamwork. There are organisation development specialists, training and personnel officers, and many other senior executives who spend a good deal of their time thinking about the human relations side of the enterprise, and what can be done to get people to co-operate, work as a team, help and bring out each other's potential.

And all this because, quite clearly, if people are prepared to work on a problem together, to work with rather than against each other, then they are much more likely to get a successful result.

All too often though, it is the very opposite that takes place. There are many good and bad reasons for this; and an examination of all of them would take us outside the scope of this book.

Often, people will not work for the good of the group as a whole, with agreed upon purposes and goals; rather they will work primarily for themselves and their own benefit, for their own 'empire', their own interest group, their own 'allies'. Efforts will then be pitted against any perceived danger from some other threatening group, even if this latter is supposedly 'on our side'. After all, much of the most vicious and cut-throat competition is found between interest groups that are supposedly co-operating with each other and working for the same cause, but which in fact have much more selfish and self-centred motivations!

I am not going to suggest that this sort of thing goes on all the time; but a good deal of what happens in a workplace setting will not make sense unless an underlying self-centredness, competitiveness, and lack of trust is recognised to be operating between supposedly 'friendly' groups. For example, how can it be that *appearances* and 'image-making' can count for so much more than actual *realities* if not for the fact that people are often more keen to be 'seen' to be doing a good job than actually doing it? And how can this be, if not for the fact that image-making is often easier, safer, less strenuous and more rewarding to the ego than actual achievement?

Of course, one way of getting a good reputation is actually to do a good job, and it will be very difficult (though not impossible) to hide real incompetence indefinitely! However, there are plenty who get on with things without 'blowing their own trumpets', and who are little noticed and appreciated; while others will make a vast mountain out of whatever little they have done, and benefit more from their public relations skills than from their actual talent.

Such selfish and self-centred behaviour is seen as morally undesirable, though we prefer to avoid thinking about how often it occurs. Even less often, though, do we notice the enormously destructive effects such behaviour has on our problem-solving abilities and general capacity to achieve whatever it may be that we set out to do.

Were we all genuinely to pull together in what we were doing then who knows what we might succeed in achieving? More often we are either openly at odds with each other or, equally often, we *pretend* that we are all one team together when we are in fact riven into any number of different factions.

Frequently it will not be in our interests openly to admit that we are taking a defensive and suspicious approach to others; and so we play-act the role of co-operative team member while all the time keeping our real intentions to ourselves. And so it is that we deceive others and they try to deceive us, and although we suspect that they are being less than honest, we collude with their game because we don't want our *own* strategems to be discovered.

Thus we go along with the clever tricks of others without actually challenging them. We look out with care and suspicion to see what game the other side are up to. But we don't openly ask "where's the catch?" "what trick is this?" since this would expose everyone to the uncharted and terrifying waters of Truth! Better, we think, to keep playing our cards as cunningly as we can rather than expose ourselves by letting our guard down. The other side would almost certainly deny that they were indulging in any kind of strategem whatever, and then, by implication, our game-playing would be revealed, while they would be continuing to pretend that they were completely 'above board' in all that they were doing. This would put us at a grave disadvantage in relation to our opponent.

Once you are clear about all this, all kinds of seemingly strange behaviour at work and among teams of any sort become clear. For example, do you know about committee meetings where everyone agrees that "great progress is being made", "we really need to meet again and develop this further", and yet precious little seems to get done compared with what is being claimed? Or work-groups and colleagues who agree that "this is an excellent proposal, we really need to give it a high priority" – and yet who never seem to manage to implement it on any significant scale?

When opposition is on the surface and openly declared, we all know where we are, and we are all clear why little progress is being made. More usually, though, the opposition, defensiveness and suspicion is kept hidden beneath the surface, and camouflaged with propaganda about co-operation. The sabotage takes place covertly, in all kinds of delicate and subtle ways. Rather than saying 'no' outright, the opponent says 'yes' but then finds all kinds of ways of de-railing, dis-empowering, deflecting, destabilising, confusing, mystifying, delaying and generally defeating the proposal, while all the time *seeming* to be moving heaven and earth to get it implemented. The greatest, most sublime versions of this creative, collective, collusive deceit take place when certain kinds of humanistic organisation development specialists move in on a workplace with the cries of "honesty, co-operation, team-building, love, mutual respect, openness" etc. People may well say "Oh yes, absolutely, the very thing we need here" and will put on a really excellent show of going along with the team spirit. But the reality will so often be quite another matter.

Don't worry about it, though, because the organisation development specialist will have strategems of his own, and will want to pretend to himself and to others that everything is going swimmingly, and so may be the last to say "fraud, pretence, deviousness; it's not working". After all, if he said that too often, his own 'empire' and reputation would be on the line, and so would be that of the people who had hired him! When it gets to be in everyone's interests to keep on with a deceit, and to keep on ensuring that everyone else keeps on doing so, then it gets very difficult indeed to break out of this game and actually face up to what is actually going on.

Some critics will say that the social psychologist too often only manages to get people to *pretend* to co-operate. Another criticism is that too many of the more individualistic approaches to psychology and psychotherapy are in effect means of encouraging selfishness (and self-centredness) in people. It might, for example, be alleged that this entire book is a means, or might be used as a means, of helping people to beome more *effectively* selfish – and never mind the wider social and moral considerations and concerns for the greater good!

If this were the case, then the whole topic of problem-solving would not be particularly worthy, worthwhile or admirable. If I thought that all I was doing was helping people to armour themselves more effectively against others, so that they could become ever more fascinated with themselves alone, and ever more skilled at outwitting and outmanoeuvering others – then this whole venture would seem to be ultimately destructive and insidious for us all.

There is a real issue here. Psychology is a study of individuals and how they function – both alone and in groups. And if the subject is to be of practical use to individuals, what are we to say when individual self-interest seems to conflict with the interest of the group as a whole, or with the wider society?

It is no use pretending that individual and group interests never conflict because, at least on the surface of things, they would appear to conflict quite substantially at times. And so, if some sort of reconciliation between self and group interests is possible, it cannot be made with a few simplistic and bland assertions that 'there is no problem here'.

Suppose that you are trying to deal with some problem in co-operation with others. The task is too big for one person alone to manage and so you need to work in conjunction with other people. If you are all selfishly competing *against* each other so that your own gain is more important to each of you than getting the job done – will this help the group to deal with the problem? . . . More often than not, it won't! And we can all, I'm sure, think of countless occasions where a group or 'team' failed to make much headway with its task beause it was so riven with the conflict between its ego-centric members.

When people are all pulling in different directions in order to further their own private schemes rather than the goals of the group as a whole – then the group task either doesn't get completed at all or, more often, gets done very badly and only after much unnecessary 'wheeling', 'dealing', scheming, 'image-making' and general delay.

Yet look what has happened here: The individual, I suggested, had joined the group in the first place because he couldn't deal with the particular problem on his own. He needed to work in a team with others in order to be able to deal with the problem at all. Yet, so often, we can forget why we came together in the first place, forget that our *longer-term* best interest lies in working together as a team, and allow ourselves to be side-tracked into individual schemes and schemings that provide a more immediate and obvious private advantage and gain. Then, when enough people in the group begin to operate along similarly selfish lines, the group-as-a-whole begins to fail in its agreed purposes, and everyone starts to be worse off, since they are driven back into the individual isolation that, they had already discovered, was insufficient to help them deal with so many of the problems they wanted to master.

"Ah yes," the cynic (and others!) will say, "that is true. If large numbers of people refuse to pull together and 'do their bit' for society then we are all likely to be worse off. But this doesn't have to happen. If *most* people co-operate more or less well, (and generally they do), then there can be enormous gains for selfish (and cunning) individuals who benefit both from the team effort *and* from their own private schemes 'on the side'."

Such an unco-operative minority can make no personal sacrifice and little contribution to the efforts of the group as a whole, but still benefit from its labours. Instead, this selfish minority puts all its energies into seeking its own private gain – even if this is at the expense of others – and so it can do very well for itself.

Of course, if such selfish behaviour becomes too visible and the destructive consequences too obvious to others, then the selfish individual is likely to lose out as a result of all the criticism, outrage and retribution from those who have been exploited. But this catastrophe need never occur if the selfish individual is sufficiently cunning. If you are smart enough, you can fool people into believing that yours is the greatest sacrifice even though in fact you have done nothing.

And so it is that there are some who fail to co-operate, who exploit others, who make enormous personal gains in addition to the benefits they receive from living in society, and are praised by others for what is believed to be their 'enormous' contribution! Moreover (such is our capacity for *self*-deception), the arch-exploiter will often even manage to convince himself that he is a great benefactor, and has made great sacrifices for the good of all!

It is not an altogether just world! And it is a fiction to say that 'crime doesn't pay'! It can pay handsomely if you are smart enough, and there are plenty who will show a craven admiration and respectful awe for displays of raw power and material success. If you are really smart, you can not only 'not get caught', you can be seen as a philanthropist rather than a criminal-at-large. And so, to take an extreme case, instead of successfully robbing a bank you can manipulate your way into owning the bank; or, rather than evading the law, you can become powerful enough to change the law to suit your own advantage. The law is then no longer an expression of an ethic that seeks to protect and support all citizens, but becomes a means of protecting the booty gained by the selfish minority.

As we look around the world, now, or at any time in the past, we see that a great deal of the 'law and order' that exists serves to defend ill-gotten gains rather than to protect individuals from exploitation. Genuine civil liberties are, and always have been, difficult to nurture and protect and, so often, the brigands and robbers, far from being controlled by the 'authorities', actually *become* the authority! (They then take upon themselves all the airs, expectations and assumptions of those who consider that they are the 'natural' governors. They become the Establishment.)

Such injustice is probably somewhat less overt and rampant in the 'civilised' West than it is in some other countries, since our own 'Establishment's' medieval roots in more blatant forms of thuggery are a long way behind it. But I would suggest that we have no cause whatever to feel easy and complacent.

Don't exploitative people suffer in the end? Don't they feel guilty at the end of the day? Are they not wracked and tortured by a gnawing self-doubt and self-disdain? Don't they have to avoid looking at themselves in the mirror?

Well, sometimes, perhaps. But we can all become very good, not only at bamboozling others into believing that we are more worthy and honourable citizens than we really are, but also in convincing *ourselves* that this is so! We can, and do, come to believe our own rhetoric; and milder versions of psychopathic behaviour are not so rare as they might seem. The psychopath, remember, loses no sleep at all over his grossly anti-social behaviour; and there are many sleeping now who we might hope would be lying awake at night plagued by their own remorse.

But surely something has died within such selfish individuals? ... a sensitivity, concern and empathy for others, a subtlety of feeling, an ability to be close and open to others? Probably this is true; if we were all able to feel and express our love and empathy for fellow mortals, then selfish behaviour that inflicted harm upon others would be anathema to us. I would experience the pain of another as though it was my own pain; and with such saint-like refinement and sensitivity, every stranger would be experienced as my long-lost brother or sister, whom I could never wish to harm.

The reality, of course, is very different, because there are not very many of such saint-like figures around! So often, precisely because such finer feelings have 'died' (or were never allowed to grow in the first place), the selfish and self-centred person doesn't necessarily suffer from their absence. We will sometimes try to engender feelings of guilt in others because of what we see as their anti-social behaviour; and we do this because we (rightly) suspect that they are not feeling guilty enough (or at all) as a result of their behaviour!

Because of our insensitivity, we may not experience the joy of knowing that everyone is my brother and sister; but neither do we suffer much remorse when we exploit our fellow mortals!

If it was obviously true that the 'meek shall inherit the earth', and that evil shall receive its just deserts – then there would be no real problem about immorality and anti-social behaviour. People would just obviously see that their own private benefits coincided exactly with the greater good, and would therefore not have much difficulty in 'being good'.

We can, of course, try to provide rewards for those who are 'good' and punishments for those who are anti-social, so that private and social gains are made to more nearly overlap. But there are severe limits to what can be done. The most effective policing took place, not in the present high-tech society – but when people were convinced in the belief that there was an all-seeing 'policeman-cum-accountant' who took careful note of every major and minor infringement, totted up the total score, was not to be bamboozled or avoided, and who meted out Big Rewards and Big Punishments at the end of our lives.

If you believe that sort of thing, then morally upright, socially co-operative behaviour does not at all clash with your own self-interest. After all, no selfish pleasures are so good as to be worth burning for eternity in a fiery furnace (except, perhaps, in the minds of a few romantics!). And so ethics, for such traditional believers, is merely a matter of delayed self-gratification, prudent self-interest; involving a refusal to indulge in immediate and obvious short-term gains in order to reap far greater personal rewards in the longer-term. 'Heaven' thus becomes that which we realise after entering into an endowment policy on earth, where there are small payments and sacrifices required in order to secure a very great long-term personal gain. In the meantime, we bow and scrape, and cringe and apologise, and generally seek to curry a few personal favours from the Almighty, and we call all this 'prayer'!

I would suggest that such beliefs in a 'Cosmic-Policeman-cum-Accountant', apart from being false, fail to come to grips with the central dilemma of ethics. Which is that just sometimes you are required to make *real* personal sacrifices even though there will be no long or short term gain for yourself, and even though you *could* get away with it if you cheated. Another myth is thus revealed: "Cheats never prosper!" They do, and they've often done very well on it! The trouble is that, if enough people cheat, then we all start to do very badly indeed. Not for the first time, there are just such fears about mass cheating around today.

When a sense of moral obligation to society decays beyond some, difficult to pinpoint, extent, we all start to quake and shiver and fear that we will all soon be in deep trouble. For when people retreat into selfish individualism, with no concern whatever for the greater good and no willingness to co-operate with others, our lives become:

"Solitary,
Poor,
Nasty,
Brutish
... and *Short*!" – as the English philosopher, Thomas

Hobbes, stated (1588–1679).

Nothing I have said here provides an easy analysis of just what *should* be an acceptable set of moral principles; of what is just and fair; and of what *should* be an acceptable balance between overly-heavy authority and overly indulgent individualism. At one extreme, individuals can be crushed by a slavish belief in the 'good of society' and, at the other extreme, society as a whole and its individual members suffer as a result of widespread selfishness and licentiousness. There is no easy way of finding the best compromise that might lie somewhere between these two extremes. It is not for nothing, or through carelessness or lack of effort, that people have written for centuries on ethical matters without achieving a once-for-all resolution. The subject is simply not open to that kind of simple answer. Part of what it is to be alive and responsible is that we confront these dilemmas throughout our lives with a substantial degree of doubt, uncertainty and conflict, both within ourselves and between ourselves and other people.

I am tempted, all the same, to suggest that those who have had a deeper sense of communion with others, a deeper understanding of their interconnectedness with others, of the joys of giving and receiving – these 'good' people have essentially been more at peace with themselves and the world than the selfish and anti-social individual who sees life as a jungle, where you defend, attack, exploit, manoeuvre, outwit and deceive other people. However, although I believe that this is true, I cannot *prove* it and, in any case, true or false, I believe that there are moral obligations regardless of whether or not we can show that ultimately they accord with our own deepest sense of well-being.

Moral obligations will remain as moral obligations regardless of whether or not people can discover, by means of them, greater peace, harmony, enlightenment – or anything else. Hence psychology ought not to replace decadent versions of religious teachings which argue that self-interest and social obligation always, and easily, overlap. Worst of all, psychology should not allow itself to become merely a tool for helping people to become more efficiently selfish or self-obsessed. The danger in psychology is that, in examining individual experience, we allow ourselves to do this in a social vacuum.

We are not totally independent and autonomous individuals, and if we just examine our own short- and long-term gains and losses without regard for the effect this has on the wider society then we create an amoral world of selfishness leading rapidly to social chaos. Some brands of popular psychotherapy do indeed seem to be in danger of being co-opted by the 'feel-good', 'joy-on-the-cheap', hedonism of (parts of) contemporary culture. This excess needs to be avoided, though without our relapsing back into yet another version of Puritanism.

Problems arising from a lack of COURAGE, LOVE and WISDOM:

44. I am too **withdrawn**.

Do you know the experience of feeling 'battered' by others? Have you been, or do you believe that you have been, betrayed, ignored, deceived, attacked, insulted, slighted, wounded, or invaded by others? Have you, in response, struck back, or shown your feelings, or found some more devious response? At other times have you thought to yourself "to hell with it, and to hell with you!" and withdrawn into yourself?

Withdrawal has its place. There are bound to be times when, for whatever reason, we are tired of the company of others, and need to retreat into our shell to rest and recharge, or take stock, or simply enjoy and learn from all those many pleasures and worthwhile moments and experiences that can only be had when we are alone. We cannot 'find ourselves' if we are *never* with others; but neither can we do so if we are *always* with them, enmeshed with them and never alone.

It may be best if we are alone with ourselves for just a few moments or sometimes, perhaps, for weeks at a time. Somehow or another we each have to find out what would be the right balance for us, and then see how far we can achieve this ideal in the everyday world of inevitable compromise. Some make the mistake of getting too enmeshed with other people, so that they never get the chance to draw back. Others withdraw and stay withdrawn in lonely isolation.

Let's be clear about this. We are essentially *social* beings, and every individual's material and psychological well-being is inextricably bound up with the well-being of society as a whole. We are not born as isolated individuals who can then decide whether and how we will negotiate our way into the social world. We are born *within* this social world. It gives birth to us and we are an expression of it, just as it becomes an expression of who we are. And so any attempt to withdraw once and for all from the world around us is based on an illusion that we can separate ourselves off, that we don't need others and they don't need us.

"A problem shared is a problem halved." – Trite, perhaps, but true. It may be that 'self-help' books like this are in demand not just because (hopefully) they may have something of value to offer, but also because there are growing numbers of people who

seem to be isolated from others and who therefore need to turn
to books and other media as a substitute for the day-to-day
ordinary human support and advice that, in a healthier society,
they would have otherwise received. If so then, let's make it
plain, books like this are *not* a substitute for ordinary human
support and advice. No doubt there are many day-to-day
problems we all face that we manage to sort out on our own,
without any contact with, or co-operation from, others.

But most of our bigger problems are not like this, and we
cannot expect to be able to make much headway with them if we
try to 'go it alone'. There is presently a fad amongst some people
for self-sufficiency and individual enterprise; but the truth,
surely, is that we cannot travel very far on our own. Those who
think they can are ignoring most of the deep-seated interconnections of mutual need and mutual inspiration that exist
among us all.

And so we may try to turn ourselves into individual islands of
isolation. But insofar as we might ever succeed in cutting
ourselves off from others to any significant extent, we will find
that our island of isolation becomes a barren desert if it gives
nothing to and receives nothing from others. Moreover, many of
the problems that we thought we would be able to tackle so much
better on our own, without interference from others, we find we
cannot tackle at all.

45. I don't **trust** others

Withdrawal and trust are closely interlinked. Often we withdraw
because we have decided that we do not trust a person
sufficiently to stay at our present distance from them. We no
longer trust that the other will support, nurture, amuse or
inspire us sufficiently for us to feel comfortable, and so we
withdraw from them in proportion to our lack of trust in them.
Sometimes, we will withdraw because we do not trust *ourselves* in

some way or another. Some measure of trust is essential if we are to be with people at all! We need both to trust ourselves with others, and trust them with us – trusting that the outcome of our meeting will not, at the very least, be too catastrophic!

Yet what exactly do we mean when we talk of 'trust'? Does it mean that I'm absolutely certain that something I might fear will not take place? If I trust you, does that mean that I trust you in every respect, and in all circumstances, to any extent? If we take such a 'black and white' approach to trust we are surely doomed to a great deal of unnecessary grief and disillusionment. And some people do indeed seem to make the mistake of going to either one extreme or the other. They will start off assuming that a person, or people in general, can be completely trusted in every way about everything. And then, when they get their fingers burnt, as they inevitably must, they are deeply shocked, mortified and undermined, so that they then go to the other extreme of trusting no one, under no circumstances, about anything.

More realistically, we need to assess just to what extent, and in what precise circumstances, we would be wise to trust specific individuals. We may trust them in some situations but not in others. And this is not to imply that we think ill of them. It simply means that we have tried to make an honest assessment of the risk in making ourselves vulnerable to them, and will act accordingly.

Even when I say "I trust you to do (or not to do)..."... whatever, this does not necessarily mean, "I am quite *certain* that you can be relied upon to live up to my trust". Rather, it means, "I am willing to take the risk and act *as though* you will not let me down".

Some will disagree with this, and suggest that trust implies that I am quite certain that you will not betray me. But I think that this is to be altogether too idealistic about the way people actually behave. Of course, you can always go around trusting everyone implicitly, taking enormous risks, and getting badly hurt for much of the time; but this seems to me to be a form of masochism!

What I am saying here does not fit in with the romantic conception, where we are supposed to trust our beloved quite without limits and without question. It is expected that we will see them as paragons of virtue and that they will blossom ever more if we remain quite unconditionally open and vulnerable to them, regardless of what they may have done in the past and might do again. Love and trust, then, the romantics will tell us, is blind, uncritical, and never operates with any degree of prudence or self-protection! This, I think, is escapist nonsense. It is something we can dream about as a light relief from the real world of compromise and limitation. But it is no recipe for survival, mutual respect and co-operation, or even a genuine love and trust!

If we can love, then we can do so despite the weaknesses of ourselves and others; but it is rather unwise of us to pretend that people do not have any weaknesses! We are all impressed by those stories of extreme heroism where a person never betrays a trust despite horrifying torture or tantalising temptation. But, let's face it, most of us are rather more in the 'middle range' when it comes to trust and reliability! We are reliable and trustworthy up to a point; but we have our limits. We can ultimately be bought or broken, if the price is high enough, the temptation great enough, or the suffering sufficiently intense.

"Horrors! Disgraceful! Cynicism!" cry the romantics. But is it cynical to be merely realistic about ourselves and our weaknesses? It is cynicism if we become scathing and contemptuous of people and their limitations. But we are more likely to do this if we start off with ludicrously high ideals which are then doomed to disillusionment in the real world. This can lead us to fall into the underlying bitterness and despair that acts as a fuel to real cynicism.

The romantic will say, "I love and trust this person absolutely. We were made for each other. We could never live without each other". The realist says, "I love this person, and I trust him very substantially, I am prepared to risk a great deal with him, but, in loving him, I know that he has his limits".

The romantic is often someone who has not yet become cynical. He or she will not live life with people as they actually are, with all their strengths and weaknesses. Rather s(he) insists on pretending that they are 'larger than life'. This reveals an ultimate lack of faith and trust in people as they really are; a preference for fantasy at the expense of reality. The trouble with illusions like this is that they lead, sooner or later, to disillusionment!

In actual fact it can come as something of a relief when we see that someone is trusting us even though they know we are not entirely trustworthy. After all, they are then more likely to be living with the truth about us, and we no longer feel that we have to put on a show for them – with all the tension that this involves. Similarly, *we* can relax, and others can relax with us, when we trust ourselves despite our limitations, and we no longer have to pretend to be greater paragons of virtue than we really are.

Once we are clear that trust involves taking a (large or small) risk (and we can each decide how big a risk we are prepared to take) we can then go ahead and not feel that it is a dreadful and surprising catastrophe if that trust is betrayed. Because it *will* sometimes be betrayed (that's what it means to be taking a risk!) and, depending on the size of the risk you are prepared to take, it will be betrayed more or less often.

You may say that, because you consider betrayal to be so terrible, you will only ever take tiny risks and will scarcely ever trust anyone. So be it! But you need to remember that, while reducing the risk of betrayal, you are *increasing* the risk of isolation and withdrawal from others. For if we are to be in any real sense with people at all, we have to let down some of our armour in relation to them, and there is bound to be a risk involved in doing this. Quite often we may not even be in a position to know how large or small this risk may be!

We just have to live with such uncertainty, and get on with action and decision-making as best we can. If you say "I'll trust when there's no risk" or "I'll trust when I know exactly what the risk is", then you'll probably never trust at all.

So far the whole discussion on trust has centred around self-interest. We trust, or not, according to implicit calculations of the risk of personal gain or loss. Yet what about the gain and loss for *others*? What about trusting because others might gain from this even though *you* might lose? (This takes us back to the discussion in section forty-three). Trust, surely, is sometimes rather more than a matter of rational (or irrational) assessment of the likelihood of personal loss or gain; it also, sometimes, involves a willingness to take a step into the unknown; to take a step, even, for *others*. And the realist, in addition to facing up to the weaknesses and failings of humanity, is also willing to accept that we also have great strengths, unused potentials, and a real capacity for genuine sacrifice and unselfishness – sometimes!

46. I am too **blaming** of others.

Oh, blame, blame, who are we to blame? Someone is to blame. Own up! "It's not me. It's him (or her)!"

Too often, when we ask, "who is to blame?" we are not simply and honestly seeking to find the cause(s) of the trouble. Rather, we are trying to take attention away from the contribution we know *we* made, and instead focus upon what other people did, or didn't, do. In other words, when we blame we tend to be looking not for *all* the causes of the trouble, but only those causes and circumstances that do not involve us!

Apart from being morally unacceptable, such behaviour reduces our ability to deal effectively with problems. After all, when things go wrong (or right!) we need to learn just how this happened; and it is no use to us if we discover only some of the reasons or give ourselves an altogether exaggerated and distorted picture of the causes at work. We cannot learn if we do not learn honestly and dispassionately from our mistakes; and we will fail collectively to tackle problems very well if we refuse to make an honest and open appraisal of what went wrong, where and why. A (would-be) 'team' in which members indulge in mutual blame and recrimination whenever the going gets tough is not likely to be very successful in tackling its problems.

When everyone is blaming everyone else, we can at least see a rich variety of possible causes being aired. But the mutual frustration, polarisation and bitterness that this leads to can be very destructive. Equally damaging are those occasions where some of the members of the group, for whatever reason, *accept* all the blame being heaped upon them, even when they are only partially responsible. The victim/scapegoat(s) may then very well bury all sorts of angry and bitter feelings about their plight; both from themselves and from others. Meanwhile the group that was responsible for scapegoating remains ignorant of what actually went wrong.

Even when we manage to find everyone who deserves some measure of blame (including ourselves!) there may still be problems. After all, what do we do then? If we learn from the mistakes that have been made, then that's fine. If we have some measure of regret about what we did wrong, then fair enough. If we feel a certain amount of guilt about our more careless and slipshod errors then all well and good. But what if we go beyond this? What if we torture and flagellate ourselves? What if we are brutal and unforgiving with ourselves (and others)? What if our conscience is a harsh and domineering tyrant, rather than a firm and supportive friend? (See section twenty-five.) Sadly, blame is too often associated with this merciless treatment of ourselves and others, and so it needs to be exercised and managed with the greatest of care.

47. I feel **bitter**.

Do you believe that you should *never* feel bitter about your mistakes and circumstances? This is scarcely realistic; and there are times when bitterness has a useful role to play. It is, after all, an extreme form of regret; about circumstances or actions, of ourselves or others. Without regrets, there would be little incentive for us to change and make changes; and in cases of extreme regret, where the feelings take on a 'bitter' taste, we have all the more incentive to take some action, to really let the lesson sink in, to really determine this time to do something.

The question, as ever in relation to very strong feelings, is: Are you going to learn from the feelings and make some corresponding changes in yourself or your circumstances? Or, alternatively, are you going to allow yourself to become paralysed, eaten up, destroyed, 'derailed', 'burned out', and (even) physically ill with them?

Take bitterness: If I feel bitter about what I have done or what others have done to me there is not much use in my repressing these feelings or being too immediately harsh on myself about them. This just becomes more of a distraction and confusion, and I find that I have not removed the strong feelings; rather I have simply over-laid them with still more strong emotions. And so, for example, I can easily find that I am not only feeling bitter; I am also feeling bitter *about* feeling bitter!

This is no word-play, and it can be very important. Many of our feelings are feelings about other feelings that we have, and, via these 'meta-feelings' (which can be as strong as, or stronger than, the original feeling) we can get ourselves into a vicious spiral of emotion so that, for example, we feel bitter-about-feeling-bitter-about-feeling bitter; or depressed-about-feeling-depressed-about-feeling-depressed; until we become thoroughly exhausted, or inactive, or despairing, or raging, or whatever.

The feelings that we have about other feelings can undoubtedly, on occasions, be much stronger than the original feelings! This happens particularly when we consider that 'we've been here before'; ie. when we feel stuck in a regular pattern of behaviour either with ourselves alone or in relation to someone else. For example, someone – say my spouse (yes, definitely my spouse!) – says or does something that I get mildly irritated about. (Never mind her irritation about me for the moment!) The feeling passes; it's not a big issue. But suppose, and this is very, very common in relation to people we live with or know well, the person has behaved in the same irritating way on 1,368 occasions in the past seven years, and every time they do it I don't like it and get mildly irritated about it?

What may well now happen is that I no longer get just *mildly* irritated. I feel irritation; and then I feel much more irritation because here I am feeling irritated *yet again* by this behaviour, and here is this behaviour, that I don't like, happening yet *again*!

And so my response is likely to be out of all proportion to what is happening because I am, in effect, responding not only to the behaviour itself but also to the memories of all the other times that this has happened. This can lead to a very large response indeed – of rage, despair, bitterness and coldness.

I am not condemning or condoning this kind of pattern of repeated sequences of behaviour and response; I am merely describing it. It *can* serve a useful purpose; emotions of any sort provide us with information about how far we like what is happening or how strongly we would prefer it to be different. With very strong 'negative' emotions we have clearly got a strong preference for something to be different, either in ourselves or in others; and so we need to ask:

1. Can I realistically make the changes that I would like to make and, if so, how?

2. Do I have the *right* to make these changes?

3. (If the answer is 'no' to either of the above): What can I do to withdraw from or come to accept the situation as gracefully as possible, so that I don't damage myself, or others, with these strong 'negative' emotions?

'Positive' emotions signal that essentially you approve of what's going on, and so the message really is "enjoy it" (while it lasts). 'Negative' emotions, on the other hand, signal that you do *not* approve (of whatever it may be – around or inside you) and the stronger the emotion the stronger the disapproval. When the message is negative (and particularly when it is strongly negative) the outcomes need to be that you take some sort of action; either to try to move away from or change what is happening; or to come to terms with it. And the stronger the 'negative' feeling the stronger and more urgent is the need for you to do something about it. If you don't, the feeling is likely to be stronger still the next time the same thing happens.

From this it should be clear that however much we may disapprove of (some) negative feelings (we may even consider them to be morally wrong) there is no use in pretending that they don't exist. They can serve a useful purpose if we deal with them wisely.

The important question is; are we going to stay stuck with these feelings and damage or destroy ourselves and other people with them; or are we going to *learn* from them, *act* upon them, and then *move on* from them? Notice that I stress the need for *action*; and the stronger the emotions the stronger the need for action. However, I am not suggesting that the action needs necessarily to be of the dramatic, running around sort. It may be best if it is far more subtle and internal; involving changes in our attitudes, intentions or expectations.

Nor do I pretend that we either *can* or *should* always get what we want! We may have strong negative emotions because we don't think we're getting what we want or need. Maybe we are not! But it's quite unrealistic to pretend that we can always get what we want, even if we do have a 'right' to it.

This is where the matter of 'bitterness' comes in. Our strongest feelings of bitterness come when we consider that we have been most unjustly treated, yet there seems to be no way out. We may be mistaken here. Maybe matters are not so unjust as we may think, and maybe we can change the circumstances that we don't like. On the other hand, maybe we can't! Furthermore, perhaps the situation is even more unjust than even *we* thought it was, and perhaps we have even less chance than we thought of changing the situation. Perhaps we have no chance at all!

If this is the case, then drastic action is needed; not action that will get us out of our predicament (because I am presently presupposing that we can't get out of it!). But action that will minimise the psychological and material damage to ourselves and other people. Action that will help us to come to terms with our predicament.

Some of the biggest changes that we can make are not external, and readily visible. They are internal and they may be difficult to notice. But they can be just as dramatic and important as more obvious public achievements. They generally involve changes in our basic attitudes to ourselves, other people and our circumstances; so that our expectations, assumptions and intentions change. Our thoughts change and influence how we feel (since feelings – contrary to popular myth – do not come and go autonomously, like the weather, but are the outcome of what we believe, want, intend, expect and perceive and interpret around us).

As we mature, the *physical* signs of our growing up are obvious for all to see, in terms of changes in one's body size and shape, one's roles in society and one's power and status. But there are, still more important, *psychological* changes that are needed if we can really be said to have grown up, involving the kinds of skills and qualities being described here. For instance, let me offer the following attitudes which can serve to reduce feelings of bitterness we may have, and which indicate that we are beginning to mature:

1. "It is a disappointment but not a catastrophe when I don't get what I want."

2. "I would be wise to work towards my ideals, but foolish to pretend that they can always be achieved."

3. "It is unwise to expect to always get what I want, and I do not always have the 'right' to get what I want."

4. "I prefer, but I don't *expect* everyone...

    ...to agree with me

    ...to like, love, approve of me

    ...to always succeed

    ...to be honest, reliable, faithful, trustworthy, interesting, willing." (etc.)

5. "I prefer, but I don't *expect*...

    ...to have a great impact on the world

    ...to become the ideal sort of person I'd like to be."

What much of this boils down to is that, if we are to avoid bitterness and really grow up, we need to learn to come to terms with ourselves and the world as it is while at the same time keeping alive our 'spark', energy and determination to make some realistic and achievable contribution. You can (try to) abandon all your ideals and expect nothing if you like, and, to the extent that you manage it, you will find some sort of peace. But in the process you will have lost your personality and humanity. You will become sluggish, fatalistic and inert.

Alternatively, you can demand too much of yourself and the world, and discover sooner or later that there are limits to what is possible and limits to your own powers of perception and judgement. If you continue to refuse to accept these limits with good grace, you will cook yourself into rage, despair and, perhaps above all, bitterness. (Maybe you have already done so?) Your whole life will become tinged by this underlying bitter taste. You will put yourself into a sulk, and these feelings will not only be highly damaging to you physically and psychologically, they will also prevent you from dealing very adequately with your problems.

In other words, in becoming bitter about not being able to do as much as you would ideally like, you will end up doing even less than you are in reality capable of doing. This can become a vicious spiral, with ever-mounting bitterness and ineffectualness feeding off each other!

The remedy is not too hard to see! But it can take a lifetime to put it into practice, and even at the very end of our days I don't suppose that any of us will have finally 'grown up'.

We never know for sure whether we are demanding too much or too little of ourselves or others. This is a source of great frustration, but it also adds to the spice, excitement and essential mystery of life! How dull it might be if we knew exactly where we were and exactly what was and wasn't possible! We would have lost the drama and adventure and, for example, no novelist could ever write a story if reader and characters were blessed (cursed) with such 'God-like' knowledge.

Bitterness is real and very common (though it is often overlaid by distractions and amusements). The young, generally, start off with grand ideals and high hopes for themselves and others. This is as it should be. But the question is, will they survive the hard realities of life that they will have to face sooner or later (these days so tragically soon). Or will they 'burn out', give up, fall down, run away, give in, over-heat, explode? – or whatever other metaphor fits for you!

48. I am **greedy**.

Greed and bitterness can sometimes be very closely inter-connected. For example, to put it crudely, a person may become bitter after their greed has not been satisfied!

Greed is at work when we start to insist that the world and other people supply us with far more than we have any right to expect and which we are quite unrealistic in demanding. However, because this is not an entirely just and fair world, people will quite often find that, in addition to being unjustly deprived, they can also be unjustly rewarded, and their greed can be satisfied even though this damages others and gives greedy individuals more than they need or deserve.

Most of us, of course, will prefer to get more rather than less than we're entitled to; and we are often very good at pretending that our greeds are really our needs. On the surface at least, the person whose greed is satisfied would appear to be luckier and more contented than the person whose need remains unmet.

In the longer run, though, the contented greedy soul is not so lucky as it might first appear. What tends to happen is that such a glutton for (undeserved) 'rewards' takes for granted what he has already received, and starts to expect and demand ever more. In this way, his expectations become ever more unreasonable. He becomes ever more greedy and ever more unaware of his greed.

Indeed, far from suspecting that he is becoming more voracious, the pampered greedy soul begins to consider that the world and other people owe him much more (than he ever originally imagined). This means that he increasingly becomes a hostage to 'good' fortune. He is ever-more dependent on things going well; ie. his well-being becomes more and more reliant on all his many greedy needs (desires) being met.

Because this can be a very unjust world, such a person may become adept at making sure that he *does* get what he wants. In particular, if we have a lot of power (for whatever good or bad reason) we will find that we can become extremely greedy – and still get away with it!

In this way, it will appear as though we have created our 'paradise' all around us, and made our dreams come true. Certainly, others may well envy us enormously! But there will be a high price that we will have to pay, whether we realise it or not – and we may very well not!

The price is that we will become ever more childish, superficial, bloated, selfish and insensitive to others. We will stay stuck at the level of the ego-centric infant, who screams when it doesn't get what it wants, and has little capacity to take any perspective on, or have any understanding of, its trials and tribulations. Such behaviour is quite understandable and unavoidable when you are two years old; but it is less than ideal when we are supposed to have grown up. The smallest set-back will send us reeling, and our dependency on the continued bountiful supply of material convenience and general good fortune will grow ever larger.

If we *never* get what we want, we face a major challenge, and we will be hard put to avoid bitterness, withdrawal and despair. If, on the other hand, we *always* get what we want (particularly when we greedily want far more than we actually need), we face a very different kind of problem.

We will dimly sense that 'this is no way to live', and we may really start to suffer from the superficiality of our lives. Tragically, however, we may fail to understand the root cause of the problem, fail to make sense of the vagueness and confusion of whatever guilty feelings we may have and instead seek to allay our unease with still more distractions and amusements. In other words, we will hide away from ourselves any latent dissatisfaction we may have with being greedy, superficial spoilt brats and we will engage in still more trivial/sophisticated pursuits and gluttonous consumption. All this will provide short-term relief but no underlying satisfaction, and no solution to the problem.

Real satisfaction can only come, not when we always get what we want (we will be unlucky if this happens), but when we manage to make a half-decent job of coping with both 'fair' winds and 'foul'! Then we shall feel that we've really 'graduated' and become 'grown up' people and fully paid up members of our society.

Some individuals remain stunted and undeveloped as persons because they have been too cruelly and unjustly treated by the world around them. Others have a very different kind of immaturity which is the result of their having been too coddled and cosseted by a world that has given them far too much of what they want; and too much to be of real value to them. People who have been bashed about by circumstances are likely, as a result, to be somewhat insensitive and unsophisticated. However, it is likely that they will be more able to cope in adversity; (because they are used to it!). On the other hand, those who have a veneer of sophistication, cultivation and maturity may in fact be hostages to (good) fortune. They may seem strong and successful, but it may be that, because of their very high expectations and the fact they have never really had to cope with serious adversities, they will collapse in a heap at the first whiff of real set-back and difficulty!

It might be reassuring to add that greedy people tend to be unpopular; that we are 'in for a fall' if we are greedy and will get our 'come-uppance'. However, although this is sometimes true I don't think it's always so. If we're successfully greedy we will find that there will be plenty of less successful, but equally greedy, admirers, who will look upon us with enormous 'respect' and envy! As I've said previously, if the morally most desirable and mature option always paid the most dividends and always overlapped completely with our own self-interest then we wouldn't have the problems that we do have with morality and maturity!

It *is* probably true that in the long run the most mature and ethically desirable approach will generally be best for us, and certainly there are many who suffer enormously because they let short-term 'comfort' triumph over longer-term well-being. But it is simplistic and inaccurate, I think, to suggest that a moral and mature path will *always* lead us to a 'happy ending'. Such a path can be difficult to take precisely because it is... difficult and (even) un-rewarding!

This gets us back to an earlier point about ethics and individualism: Greed, and the other vices, are wrong not just because they are generally not in our own individual best interests. They are wrong because they cannot conceivably operate as acceptable or workable rules governing behaviour in any sort of society anywhere. Virtue may often lead to its own reward, and it can be seen as being its own reward. But the whole point about virtuous behaviour is that we ought to practise it regardless of whether or not it provides us personally with rewards!

49. I need to be less **domineering**, spiteful, revengeful and malicious.

I think that similar considerations apply in relation to these other vices. They will all tend to lead us to be thoroughly disliked by those around us – since very few people *like* to be the victim of any of these impulses! This is important, given that so many of our problems need to be tackled as a co-operative effort with other people. After all, this kind of selfishness and self-preoccupation is a very poor basis for a co-operative team effort! Furthermore, such destructive emotions damage not only other people and our relationships with them; they also damage ourselves, because spite, malice and revenge give us an ever more jaundiced perception of other people and our predicament generally. Such emotions lead us to chronic tension, defensiveness, and angry, bitter feelings; and all this is exhausting, dispiriting and bad for our health. Such negative feelings destroy more subtle, joyful, hopeful, outgoing and sensitive perceptions and tendencies.

Again, though, let it be clear, such feelings would still be seen as wrong even if they were *not* so self-destructive and self-defeating. Regardless of whether or not we find virtue to be workable and vice to be self-defeating, the latter is still unworkable and unacceptable from the point of view of society as a whole and from the standpoint of our collective effort to deal with the problems that we all share.

50. I need to be more **patient**.

We are not going to get all that we want and, equally certain, even when we *do* get it, we will often find that we have to wait for much longer than we would have preferred!

Patience, of course, is all about coming to terms with this (yet another) limitation on our preferences imposed by reality. If we really do find that something cannot be achieved as quickly as we would like then, as ever, the wise move is to accept this with good grace, so that we avoid all the diversion, distraction and destruction of ourselves, others and our relationships that would otherwise take place.

Here, then, is another balancing point that needs to be found. We can lack patience, undoubtedly. But we can also be *too* patient, and hang around meekly, accepting and failing to be assertive in circumstances where, if we had been more 'pushy', we might have got things done much more quickly and effectively – to the benefit of all concerned. Equally certain, though, if we are insufficiently patient we will bring harm to ourselves at the very least if not to others. So, not only is it a virtue – a good moral principle – it is also a good practical rule that helps us to make an effective job of our problems.

Hopefuly the distinction between 'moral principle' and 'practical guide to problem-solving' is no longer so large as it might at first have seemed. Indeed, let me suggest the following as a working definition: A moral principle is a useful practical rule by means of which we can *collectively* deal with the problems we share. In other words morality is concerned with the matter of problem-solving at the level of society as a whole. This provides no final account of morality or society; but it does spotlight the way in which problem-solving and ethics are inextricably linked.

51. I need to **stand up** for myself; I am not sufficiently assertive.

When you feel frustrated, angry, or bitter is this due mainly to the obnoxious people or terrible circumstances you face? (We would all prefer other people to change in all kinds of ways!) Or are you in fact angry, frustrated or bitter, first and foremost, with *yourself* – for not coping with the person or situation as you would have liked? Over and over again, we will direct strong emotion outwards towards others when we are mainly seething with *ourselves* because we are dissatisfied with the way we have responded.

We can look upon our lives in all kinds of ways: Here, I want to compare it with a game of cards . . .! In life, as in cards, we can get a 'rotten' hand and we can easily pretend that our distress is entirely the result of our bad luck. But much of our frustration is due to the quality of our play rather than the indifferent value of the 'cards' we have been dealt. We are likely to feel much better about a 'bad' hand well played than a very 'lucky' hand that we have played very poorly.

We probably cannot change other people and the world around us very much, any more than we can change our luck in cards. We can, however, learn to 'play our hand' a little more effectively. If we could learn to do this, we could feel rather more satisfied with ourselves, regardless of our terrible luck! How, though, can this be done?

The first major obstacle that many of us need to deal with is our belief about ourselves! So often we take the view that we don't have the *right* to express ourselves – our own thoughts, feelings and wishes – unless others have given us 'permission'. This paralyses us from the start since we spend so much time checking that others will *approve* of what we want to say or do. We inhibit ourselves if there is any hint that our opinions, feelings or actions are not O.K.

Sometimes, we will know in our hearts that we have as much right to speak and act as anyone else; but at a more deep-seated level we do not live by, and act on, this belief. It is not really a part of our lives. It can take years of practice, reminders and (preferably) encouragement from others, before we are really able to 'speak out' and 'step forward'.

This reluctance to speak up and slavish concern for the approval of others is often caused by an underlying insecurity and low self-esteem. The non-assertive person will have a tendency to feel excessively guilty and regretful about much of what she does, and consequently she will find it very difficult to stand up for herself against anyone who happens to conflict with her about anything. All her 'opponent' needs to do is undermine her (already low) self-esteem, and encourage her to feel guilty, stupid or uneasy. Given that she is already prone to excessive guilt and insecurity, such an undermining process will be relatively easy. She will quickly fall into line with what the other, more dominant, individual wants, thinks or feels.

People so often tend to take extreme positions; and drive each other into opposite extremes. And so, if one person is feeling that she needs 'permission' from others to speak, think and feel at all, her 'opponent' is likely to be considering that what *he* prefers, or feels, or believes in, is sanctioned by God, morality or any other would-be objective standard.

It is then very tempting for the dominant person to say, not simply: "This is what I think/feel/want (but you may see it differently)"; rather, he says "This is right/good/proper/decent/ necessary/absolutely true; and if you see it any differently you are stupid/wrong/wilful/sinful and you should feel uneasy/guilty/ regretful". In other words, we don't 'come clean' with people and say "I want you to fit in with what I want"; rather, we pretend (to ourselves and to others) that what we want is "right/good/proper/decent/necessary/absolutely true."

Moral principles are very important, but we all have a tendency to dress up our own detailed personal perceptions and preferences as though they really were moral 'absolutes'. We then proceed to try to undermine people who won't fit in with us. This pseudo-moralisation is in itself immoral, and it certainly leads to a complex web of dishonest strategems, as each 'side' tries to undermine the other, while all the time denying that they are doing any such thing. Truth gets quite lost in this psychological warfare, and propaganda becomes all. Sadly we even have a tendency to become convinced by our own propaganda – which takes us still further away from any sort of objective picture of what is actually going on.

There are many ways of preying on people's latent unease, guilt and uncertainty. Nobody likes to make mistakes, be unclear, confused, contradictory, equivocal, or ignorant; and no one likes to appear to be selfish, self-centred, insensitive, or stupid. And so the anxious, uneasy, guilty sort of person will have great difficulty in asserting herself, particularly against a manipulative, or bullying, 'pseudo-moralist'; because as soon as he even hints that she is in any way mad, bad or stupid she will tend to believe these charges. She will then almost immediately try to fit in with his preferences and perceptions in order to regain his approval or, at least, avoid his wrath and/or moral condemnation. (In this illustration I am referring to 'he' as the *predator* and 'she' as the *victim*. There are, of course, one or two predatory and manipulative females around as well; and some males who adopt the role of 'passive victim'!)

In the short run, this sort of grovelling works for the non-assertive, deferential, 'victim'. It at least gives her respite from the other person's disapproval and her own self-doubt. But in the longer run she is likely to get more and more resentful of this pseudo-moralist (or bully), and more and more angry and frustrated with herself for her own failure to deal with him. She loses whatever respect for herself she may have preserved; and the successful manipulator loses respect and regard for such a 'doormat'; despite (*because of*) all her desperate efforts to please him.

Low self-esteem leads to a lack of assertiveness; which lowers your self-esteem still further; which means you are even less likely to be assertive – and so on. Another vicious sequence.

If you are lacking in assertiveness, then you need to carefully examine the way the process works in your own life (preferably with the help and support of others). After that it is a matter of practice, practice and more practice in order to break out of the vicious cycle and establish a more positive sequence where small efforts to assert yourself raise your self-esteem, thus helping you to make a slightly bigger effort next time – and so on. There is bound to be a good deal of trial and error, and you have to be content with small, step by step, improvements, and patient about the many set-backs that are bound to occur.

Eventually it becomes possible for you to express your feelings without either repressing them or exploding with them. (The explosion of emotion is generally a consequence of chronic repression.)

Do you believe that you have a right to hold, and to express, your own thoughts, feelings and preferences if you so choose; regardless of whether or not others approve or agree with them? If you don't, then you will have handed your power to others who, in your view, must give you 'permission' before you can speak or act at all. This may well mean that you feel powerless; but, don't forget, it was *you* who gave this power away, and thus it is you who can take it back again, any time you choose.

Perhaps you are the sort of person who believes that you should keep quiet unless, and until, you are absolutely certain, correct, convinced, convincing, consistent, clear, coherent, concerned and competent in your views or feelings! Clearly, if you wait until you reach such absolute certainty you are likely to have to wait forever!

There may quite often be occasions when we decide to withhold our own opinions and feelings because we think that it will be in our own, or another's, or everyone's, best interests if we keep things to ourselves. After all, honesty and directness are virtues; but so too are tact, sensitivity and goodwill!

However, when we *do* decide to 'keep our own counsel' it is important that we are clear about our motives. If we genuinely believe that we are doing 'what is best' then fair enough. But what if we are keeping quiet because of fear of the consequences?

If this is the case, are we wise to let this fear govern our activities? Possibly we are – at least for the time being! Possibly, though, we are letting fear govern our lives, and maybe we don't even believe that we have any *right* to assert ourselves. If so, then we might be wise to face up to these underlying motives and see if we can, gently but firmly, change both the beliefs and the hesitant, unassuming, deferential 'mouse-like' behaviour that follows on from them.

We will find that some people will not like what we say and do (we can't please everyone!), and we are sometimes going to have our own regrets. We are frequently going to be inconsistent, inaccurate, incomprehensible, incorrect, incoherent, and/or insensitive. We may try to avoid all these 'faults' but, being human, we are bound to fail – regularly! We don't have to let other people exert moral blackmail over us because of this; and we don't need to believe that others are 'paragons of virtue' in all these respects; however much they may pretend otherwise!

Essentially, in the long run, we will get more respect from other people when we are prepared to assert ourselves – even if this does mean that they are sometimes surprised, or shocked, or irritated with us. We will get *most* respect and appreciation from others, though, if we can both assert ourselves, tactfully, and encourage others to do the same!

The trouble, so often, is that people tend to 'specialise' in just one or the other of these qualities and skills. And so you will find some people who are most keen to state their position, make themselves heard, be listened to, stand their ground etc. – and they can become very good at doing all this. However, because they don't allow others the same rights, they are recognised as selfish, demanding, domineering and thick-skinned. There may be a (grudging) respect (even envy) for their self-assurance and their insistence on being heard, but there will also, under-standably, be a good deal of resentment, irritation and positive dislike for their selfishness.

At the other extreme, are those who put most of their time and energy in 'being there' for others. They are good listeners, they are careful in their attempts to see how things look 'from other people's shoes'. They try to fit in and make people happy. All very fine, and we all like to have people show such concern for us and interest in what we think, feel and want.

But if these caring, supportive, sensitive people are not also prepared to state their own views, defend their own integrity and 'make a few waves' sometimes then it is likely that they will be taken for granted by others, treated like doormats, and generally not shown sufficient respect.

Moreover, in the long run, it is very frustrating and irritating to be with someone who only ever listens to you but who never wants you to listen to them. We feel either that they are patronising us in some way – like the 'father'/'mother'/'counsellor' figure who listens to you so that you can sort yourself out but who never needs you to listen to them! Or, more likely, we think that such a person is looking *up* to us too much, and being too craven, deferential and fearful of us. We don't feel that we can get through to them because they won't let themselves come through to us. In other words, for all that they really will listen to us, we feel frustrated because they don't give *us* a chance to listen to them.

Ultimately, we feel more connected to people to the extent that we can both give to and receive from them a rich variety of messages – ranging from the profound to the whimsical. Messages, moreover, that come from the heart rather than just 'plastic', devious, manipulative, tactical presentations.

Most important of all, being more assertive should not be about winning more battles, putting one over on one's 'opponent', standing one's ground come what may, bulldozing or steam-rolling other people. This narrow vision of assertiveness involves a stubborness, selfishness and an ego-centred attachment of one's own views that gives the whole business of being assertive a bad name!

So often, the strong, assertive person is seen as the one who won't budge, who won't give in, who will stay like a rock, unmoved and unmoveable, regardless of whatever is thrown at him. Yet far greater strength, surely, is needed if we can assert ourselves while at the same time being sensitive, tentative, tactful, flexible and willing to compromise. In other words, if we can state our own views, feelings and wishes with goodwill and a genuine regard for the feelings, thoughts and wishes of other people.

Of course, it is often difficult to know if we have got the balance right. Sometimes we are not sure whether we are being too invasive of other people or too willing to let them 'invade' our own privacy or integrity. At least, though, if we are genuinely trying to operate with respect and concern for ourselves and others, we can at least know that our 'heart is in the right place' and that there is goodwill in what we do. Then, although we are bound to make mistakes and go on making them however much we try, we can at least honour and respect our good intentions. (These may not in themselves be adequate, but they are at least a step in the right direction!)

Assertiveness, then, requires both courage and wisdom. Courage, in order to face up to people and live through hostility, resentment and opposition to what we believe we must stand for and defend. But wisdom, in order to know when it would be best to avoid 'making an issue' of something. We will run into trouble if we are never prepared to stand up for ourselves. But we will also get into all kinds of unnecessary pain and confusion if we feel that we must 'bang our drum' about every matter, and every injustice, that presently concerns or preoccupies us. If we do this, others will rightly see us as being too self-obsessed, self-preoccupied, perfectionistic, demanding, inflexible, uncompromising and unrealistic. We need to know *both* when to speak out, stand our ground and make a stand; *and* when to shut up, let the matter pass and let go of our feelings. We are bound to get it wrong a lot of the time. A great deal of trial and error here is inevitable.

We all want to be heard by others, and we will not be heard if we are not prepared to speak out sometimes. On the other hand, people will be reluctant to listen if we shout at them aggressively, or try to bully or manoeuvre them into listening. They will also be reluctant to listen if we don't show an equal willingness to listen to them.

Even if we manage to do all of this it may still not be enough! I have seen people fail to communicate because they are deferential and quiet, and fail because they are loud and domineering (or manipulative). Equally important, I have seen failures to communicate because people have not been willing to help each other to protect their own self-esteem; to 'save face'. (Many of these latter failures have been my own!)

Nearly all the literature that I have seen on the subject of assertiveness focuses too much on awareness of "me and what I need" and scarcely at all on "you and your needs". Apart from being self-centred and selfish, this attitude does not ultimately help you to be very assertive. After all, none of us are very keen to listen to, and take an interest in, other people and their needs if they show no sign of being (genuinely) interested in us and ours.

We all of us would like to feel O.K. about ourselves; and so we prefer to be reassured, rewarded and supported by others rather than undermined, punished and attacked. The pseudo-moralist will try to show that the other person is wrong by dressing up his own preferences as though they were moral principles. But what if the other person really *is* wrong? Even here, surely, tact, sensitivity and face-saving formulae are to be preferred. Because:

a. It is morally desirable, since the 'face-saving' approach shows respect, mercy, compassion, tact and sensitivity.

b. We are much more likely to be heard, respected and appreciated if we help the other person in this way. Moreover, we are then more likely to be able to find a mutually acceptable compromise.

It has become rather unfashionable, in the West, to consider the importance of 'saving face'. The style of communicating that goes in for face-saving formulae is seen as dishonest, weak-willed and inauthentic; a wily oriental means of communicating! The virile Westerner, graduate of Assertiveness Training Courses, will have none of this. S(he) has learned to stand on his/her own two feet and others must learn to do the same – without crutches and complicity on our part.

Now, it has to be admitted that we can, in the name of tact and sensitivity merely collude with a person's lies and rationalisations; and thus protect their self-esteem by encouraging them to live in a world of illusion. This is the genuine concern of those who want to 'rip the masks away' and 'tell it like it is'! But it *is* possible, though often difficult, to be tactful without being dishonest (see section fifty-four on 'honesty'). The key to being tactful is awareness of self-esteem and its importance.

All too often the (would-be) assertive person is very aware of, and very keen to protect, his own self-esteem; but indifferent to, and oblivious of, the self-esteem and self-respect of others. Too many of the training programmes that I have seen on

Communication Skills and *Encounter* pay scant attention to this! Yet look at the consequences if you are *not* willing to (uncondescendingly!) help a person to protect his self-esteem:

Let us suppose that you have offered the person no way of saving face, no way of building on his/her own insights and skills, no possibility of 'give and take'. You offer just one option. Yours! The 'One and Only' Right answer! You want the other person simply to accept unconditional surrender, and you give him/her no room to manoeuvre. Let us suppose too that you do all this in a perfectly reasonable, calm manner so that you cannot even be accused of being aggressive or bullying!

This may sound like a marvellous victory. The stuff of our dreams. The position of effortless dominance that we would dearly love to achieve. But the skillful and systematic humiliation of our 'adversary' is both morally wrong and ultimately self-defeating. It is all the more destructive if we successfully manage to cover up from ourselves and our victim(s) the fact that we have so humiliated them!

Such (merciless) behaviour produces a sworn opponent who will be itching to get revenge on us, who will be reluctant to show us any charity, who will energetically celebrate our every mistake and misfortune. If they surrender to us they will be seething with resentment, and if we don't present them with reasonable means of protecting their own self-esteem they will be likely to choose quite unreasonable methods, like raw violence, hysteria, aggression, lies – anything at all!

We all of us have a need to preserve whatever self-respect and self-esteem we may have, particularly when so many of us feel so chronically short of these! This is a 'Truth' that is more important to us than the 'truth' of other people's assertions. We need to show real respect for this if we are to explore the truth about anything with other people.

Here, at last, we are getting to the root of what I think is a Major Human Tragedy!...

Whenever we feel threatened and hurt by other people we generally respond by being threatening and hurtful to them. We do this in either overt or cunning ways, and we usually fail to see how we have been trampling on our (would be) aggressor. We also fail to see how the aggression and unreasonableness of others is (like ours) rooted in their own insecurity and pain.

Insecurity leads to aggression ("self-defence") which leads to more hurt, pain and insecurity. This is followed by still more retaliation ("self-defence"). Eventually, everyone's self-esteem becomes badly damaged.

Worse still, everyone's lack of trust and insecurity leads them to behave in a way that justifies this lack of trust and insecurity...

We feel threatened, insecure and hurt.

We 'defend' ourselves in ways that are seen by others as an 'attack'.

They then feel threatened, insecure and hurt.

They then defend themlselves in ways which seem to us to be aggressive.

We then feel still more threatened, insecure and hurt.

And so round and round we go in this vicious sequence!

In other words, our insecurity leads to negative perceptions which result in behaviour that turns these perceptions into self-fulfilling prophesies!

If, as a result of my insecurity, I take the view that another person is a threat to me, I will start to treat them as though they were such a threat. I will generally do this by overtly attacking or more covertly undermining them. They will then feel threatened and hurt and will defend themselves by attacking and under-mining me. I will then say to myself, "Yes, I was quite right to see this person as a threat!"

In other words, if I treat someone as a threat, using my habitual methods, then they will, in order to defend themselves, actually become precisely the threat I (perhaps erroneously) believed them to be!

There is a vitally important consequence of all this. Namely, if I am to be more secure in relation to another person it should be my major priority to try to *reassure* this person; to make him feel more secure; to help him feel good about himself. When he sees me as a friend rather than a threat then he will not feel so much in need to attack or undermine me!

Tragically for us all, we generally do precisely the opposite. In order to protect our own self-esteem and sense of security we tend to undermine that of others. We imagine that if we can drive off, trip up, or outmanoeuvre other people (groups or nations) they will be less dangerous to us. In fact they will become *more* dangerous.

This tragic pattern of behaviour can be observed at every level of human contact: between individuals, groups, organisations and whole nations. Every country has a Defence Department. (Nearly) everyone considers that we are safer, if others feel less secure and less confident than we do. (Nearly) everyone likes to feel that they are a 'winner' (at the expense of other people's confidence and self-esteem); we fail to consider how dangerous it is to produce 'losers'.

Let us never forget it: the most arrogant, domineering, ego-centred, aggressive individual is suffering from... low self-esteem! He believes that he is worse than he really is, and this is why he keeps on needing to prove that he is better than he actually is. He requires enormous compassion if he is ever to be able to face himself 'warts and all'. Yet, because of the pain he inflicts on others, and their consequently feeling that they need to defend themselves, he is likely to be a target of many people's aggressive and hostile intentions and malevolent dreams.

It is so much easier to destroy than to build. So easy to damage a person's self-esteem, easy to hurt them, betray their trust, be defensive, see ourselves as separate from and at odds with others, easy to ignore how they are feeling and how they see things. And, the more hurt we feel, the easier it is to lash out in revenge, while feeling ever more right and justified in doing so. If we are ever to get out of this prison, we need to see beneath the appearances and face the enormous insecurity, low self-esteem and uneasiness that is felt by (virtually) everyone! I include myself, of course.

I want to take one more example of such self-defeating behaviour...

Generally speaking, when people talk about the value of being more assertive, they focus on the supposed importance of holding on to their positions – their opinions, feelings, thoughts, and wishes – and defending these against the attacks of others. Successful assertiveness is then seen as the process of holding on to my position while, hopefully, 'capturing' yours.

Our positions, then, are considered to be crucial 'fortresses' that the assertive person needs to protect and defend at all costs. Our integrity and self-esteem get welded to our position. If we lose the position we feel that we have lost some of our integrity and self-esteem. It is all very militaristic!

We believe that our sense of self is buttressed and supported by the positions we take; that these are like secure fortresses that help us to feel safe in this dangerous world. The more we can keep and hold on to our positions, the more 'full of ourselves' and safer we believe ourselves to be. Persons who cannot defend and maintain their positions are seen to be tragic souls indeed.

In fact we are not fortified by the positions we take; we are imprisoned or gaoled within them! They *trap* us rather than *free* us! They make it almost impossible for us to see the other person's point of view and impossible for us to negotiate flexibly. As a result of them we tend to see any disagreement or conflict as an 'either-or', 'win-lose', 'my way or your way' encounter that leads us to feel ever more stuck, blocked and insecure.

Positions are taken to be so terribly important but they are not really important at all. We only think they are important because our perception is so superficial. What really matters are not the positions we take but the (largely unmet) desires and needs that led us to adopt the position in the first place.

If we can start to engage with the underlying needs that people have, we then get beyond the mere superficialities of disagreement. We can begin to try to meet (everyone's) needs rather than defend (our) position. And we can do this both for selfish and altruistic reasons. Selfish: "You are more likely to try to meet my needs if I try to meet yours". Altruistic: "It is *right* to care for the needs of others."

Most important, because of the large variety of needs that we all have, we can begin to see that there is plenty of room for us to negotiate, compromise, give and take and create new opinions where everyone can benefit. We thus escape from the imprisoning perception of 'either this or that', 'either me or you', 'either my way or your way', 'either win or lose'.

A final word on assertiveness. Some people are most keen to assert their *opinions*, and they see this as the most important part of life and of who they really are. The positions they take are generally (much cherished) ideas! Others want to assert their *feelings*, and imagine that the world of feeling is the real world; the 'bottom line'; 'where it's really at'; the final truth about themselves. Their feelings become the precious fortresses that need defending.

Those in the first category push too hard to let you have their opinions, and tend to spend too much time 'in their heads'. Most of their time and attention is given over to their ideas. At the other extreme are those who want to know how everyone *feels* first and foremost; in the belief this is what 'real' communication is all about. Emotions, this latter category of people believe, are the bottom line that underly all thoughts and opinions. What you *think* is held to be mere superficiality; an intellectual diversion and distraction that takes us all away from the underlying reality of . . . our emotions!

Quite a number of the 'crossed wires' that occur when people try to 'get through to each other' arise from these differences of opinion and feeling about thoughts and feelings. It is easy to believe that the other person is 'essentially more superficial than I' if they have different opinions from ourselves about what is most real. And so we have the accusation – "she never says what she actually *thinks*, or even seems to care about it; she just laughs, or cries, or smiles, or frowns. I don't know where I am with her; she just won't be serious and won't talk about what's really important". And equally, the response comes: "He just lives in his head. He has an opinion about everything but I never really know how he *feels*. He talks a lot about everything, but I never know where I really am with him. And when I show how I feel he just dismisses it, ignores it or moves away still more into his head."

Of course, I am caricaturing two extreme positions here. More often, people are not poles apart, but sufficiently different in their assessment of the relative importance of thought and feeling for the differences to create problems in communicating with each other. More often than not, people will be good at asserting (communicating) thoughts *or* feelings, rather than both.

The truth, in my opinion, is that thought does not underly feeling any more than feeling underlies thought. Rather, both are always operating at the same time and are so much interconnected as aspects of our personality that it cannot be said that one 'precedes' the other. They are each cause and effect of the other, and neither can, or does, operate in isolation. We are, after all, one organism, not two.

The person who stresses and attends to only his thoughts, or only her feelings will become ignorant of how the other works, and thus less able to control, understand or recognise its importance. Thus it is that the 'thinking' sort of person will so often be subject to feelings that he is quite unaware of; and, because he is unaware of them, these feelings will become far more powerful, controlling and important than they would otherwise have been. The intellectual will thus rationalise, manipulate and manoeuvre, and much of the time fail to see this and fail to see how it is being influenced by his emotions. Moreover, the more he denies, ignores and covers up his feelings, the more important, controlling and demanding they will become, and the greater his need to rationalise and distract himself.

Equally, the person who stresses the importance of feeling will tend to be governed by opinions and beliefs that remain unexamined and unexpressed. Moreover, because the opinions are hidden and unexplored, they are likely to be rather crude, simplistic, ill thought out and inadequate.

We can only be authentic if we are aware of, and express both our thoughts and our feelings, and thus come to learn how each enriches the other. Unexpressed, unexamined, unexplored and unconscious thoughts or feelings tend to be infantile, rigid, unsophisticated, one dimensional, raw, crude, inappropriate, unhelpful and even destructive. We fail to learn from them, they are all the more powerful *because* we are ignoring them, and we fail to refine and develop them. Thus we remain rather immature, self-centred and childish in our ideas, emotions, experience and behaviour.

Two extreme examples of this: the third rate academic discussion where opinions are given by 'disembodied heads', with no interest in the connections between thought, feeling and action; or, on the other hand, the third rate 'encounter' group, where crude and infantile displays of emotion are indulged in without any attempt to understand what all this might mean within the group and the wider society, nor any concern to see what is appropriate or desirable.

52. I need to learn how to **deal with conflict**.

We are bound to be in conflict with people at times. We are bound to think and feel differently from other people and, most crucially, to have conflicting plans and schemes. Conflict can scare us, though, because we are so frightened of its destructive effects. This is not surprising because, sadly, we are so often very destructive in the way we handle conflict.

The trouble, essentially, is that too often we fail to handle our disagreements with an underlying goodwill. We don't say, "O.K., I respect your right to see it differently and to want different things". We don't try to see how matters look from another perspective, and we are reluctant to make compromises, or even to look very actively for them.

Instead, we tend to see the other person as mad, bad and wrong; who needs to be straightened out (by us!); enlightened and put on the 'right' path (the one we want and believe in!). Conflict then is seen as being about educating the other person – who is, of course, considered to be ignorant. *We* are the one with vision; *we* are the moral teacher; we are the 'good person'. This 'opponent' is deluded, confused, stubborn, ignorant, wilful, wrong, guilty and wicked. And the more wrong and wicked we think (s)he is, the more we believe that any (devious) means are justified in achieving our morally desirable ends. Consequently, we will be prepared to employ subterfuge, aggression, moral blackmail, and basically any kind of devious or undermining or offensive tactic that, we believe, might help us to 'win the day'.

Conflict, in other words, becomes a matter of winning or losing and, at all costs, we believe we must win. Our moral principles, our sense of justice and personal integrity are, we believe, at stake. We almost always think that we are fighting a 'just' war; God, morality, justice (etc.) is on our side.

No wonder, then, that with friends in particular we shy away from disagreement. We feel that if we are in conflict with our friends then our friendship will probably be damaged. And, given the destructive way in which we handle conflict, our fears are, sadly, all too often justified.

Consequently friendships are all too often shallow and brittle affairs; where a friend is someone who "allows and accepts my pretences and rationalisations as long as I allow and accept theirs". In other words, in friendship we implicitly say, "You go along with my rubbish and I'll go along with yours".

This is reassuring enough in the short run. We all like people to agree with us and to support our beliefs and actions. But we can't get into a deeper relationship with ourselves and others if we are never prepared to actually engage with and explore our differences of opinion, feeling and desire.

For a friendship to begin we are going to want to explore the ways in which we see eye to eye with others; to see how we agree with others and share similar tastes and preferences. But, if the friendship is to deepen, we have got to be prepared to deal with, and come to terms with, our differences, and to look at the negative feelings and interchanges that exist in our dealings with each other. Otherwise our connections with others will remain limited and superficial. In the longer run, if *all* our friendships are superficial, we will find this to be frustrating and unsatisfying.

We can give and receive support from others if we *agree* with them; but deeper levels of co-operation and support are possible if we can also share our *differences* without trying to attack, or defeat, or undermine each other.

Some people slavishly avoid conflict and, as a result of this, are exploited by others and lose their own, and other people's, respect. Others charge in to every disagreement and difference of opinion in a militaristic fashion; and lose out because of their self-righteousness and lack of goodwill. Neither approach is of much use in the long run, and neither is necessary.

We would all of us be able to manage conflict more effectively if we became more aware of the hurt and insecurity that usually lie beneath the surface 'armour' of both ourselves and our (potential) opponent.

Given our insecurity, we can easily imagine that others are threatening us even when they are not. Our own fear prevents us from seeing theirs, and their efforts to protect themselves are seen by us as a menace. In self defence we try to undermine or attack the opposition (in however subtle a way) and thus make them feel still more insecure. They then respond with similar undermining or aggressive tactics.

In no time at all the situation may have deteriorated from one where each party *believed* the other to be dangerous to the more painful, hurtful position where each side *really is* beginning to threaten the security or self-esteem of the other.

It is important to see that, when we are insecure, we can feel threatened by others regardless of whether or not they actually are seeking to undermine us. For example, if we meet someone who is (or seems to be) more confident and competent than us, we can find this very (appearance of) confidence threatening! We fear that we will have no chance against this 'superior' individual if we were ever to conflict, and we sense that they can see into us and our weaknesses (regardless of whether or not they can actually do so).

Consequently, we may well be tempted to try to 'pull them down a peg or two' in order to try to secure our own position. We will generally be very subtle in the way that we do this, and we may well be quite unaware of what we are doing! Before we know where we are, we may have got ourselves into an actual conflict with the person as a result of our subtle 'pre-emptive strike' designed to secure us against such conflict! And so, in order to make a person less of a threat to us, we behave in such a way that they respond by really seeking to threaten us!

This self-defeating pattern of behaviour occurs between individuals, groups and whole nations...

* We feel insecure and threatened.

* We fail to notice that the 'other side' feels the same.

* We each deny our own, home-grown, insecurity and instead focus on the (would be) threat of our opponent.

* We put on a tough, competent, confident exterior and the other side does the same. Both sides find this threatening.

* If the other side differs from us in appearance, life-style, values, beliefs etc. we find the differences that we don't understand even more threatening.

* If our opponents have different positions from ourselves we may well find these very differences threatening to our own positions.

* We look for subtle ways of undermining the confidence and self-esteem of the other side in order to secure our own position. They do the same to us. This really is threatening to each side.

★   We each slip into more overt aggressive, undermining and defensive styles of behaviour.

★   Consequently, each side feels increasingly threatened, hurt and undermined by the manoeuverings of the other. This leads to a vicious spiral.

★   We fear our neighbours, friends, partners, enemies but we daren't tell them. If we could be more open about our fears we could find compassion for each other and a release from our own tension. When will we get ourselves out of this descending spiral?

(See also section fifty-one, above.)

53. I have been very **unlucky.**

'Lady Luck'. What can we do about her? Is there anything we *can* do? What do we mean by 'luck'?

Quite often we put things down to ('good' or 'bad') luck when it is really more a question of (good or bad) judgement, skill or information. There are probably countless occasions where what we imagine to be a shortage of luck is in fact some failing or deficiency on our part.

Yet are we to say that there is no such thing at all as 'bad luck' or misfortune? People tend perhaps to talk too much of 'luck' when they would be wiser to look more at themselves, their own motives, intentions, conflicts, behaviour and history.

However, there is a (growing) minority who go to the other extreme and who will have no truck with 'luck' at all. Life, in their view, never has any chance elements in it. It may *appear* that there is bad luck but, they claim, if we did but know it, we would never see that we are *always* responsible; that there are *never* any accidents or misfortunes. "Nature", they argue, "is never indifferent or impersonal, but always makes a personal effort to teach us." According to this view, everything that happens arises from our present or previous intentions, motives, actions, perceptions and purposes. And if anything bad or unlucky or unfortunate occurs it must be the result of some present or previous failure to perceive or act skillfully or lovingly enough.

All bad news is thus seen as some kind of retribution, punishment or lesson for us resulting from some failing or limitation in ourselves.

It seems irresponsible if we ascribe all our woes to 'bad luck'; but we are having delusions of grandeur and placing ourselves too much at the centre of the universe if we believe that the whole of life is, can be, should be, or needs to be organised so as to provide us with just rewards or punishments for every great or small action we take.

Why on earth should the world gear itself around us in this way? And what evidence is there that Nature always works in such just and fair ways? It seems more likely that, for example, the proud and arrogant do sometimes but not always receive their 'banana-skin' come-uppance; and that the humble and honest toilers do sometimes but not always receive their just reward. If it was always *certain* that such morally good or bad behaviour inevitably reaped its 'just' and 'fair' return, then we would not have much difficulty in doing good. Moral action would always coincide with self-interest.

Clearly, it is often difficult to know how far our problems are the result of bad luck or bad judgement; and too many of us blame 'luck' when it was more a matter of our lack of judgement and mistaken actions.

Even when there is a good deal of luck involved, of course, this does not mean the situation was uncontrollable or inexplicable. Often, the bad luck will be the result of someone else's failure of judgement, action or perception. But, whatever the reason, we will surely call it 'bad luck' when something painful, destructive or unpleasant occurs that we took reasonable precautions to avoid.

We are all of us bound to take (generally small) risks all the time and every day of our lives. The more simple and obvious examples are those risks we take where our own physical safety is threatened. We can never be 100% safe! A plane might crash on our house while we are in it. There are small, but real, risks of our being crushed, run down, shot, infected or poisoned; and, while we can take all reasonable precautions, we don't want to become excessively cautious, obsessive or paranoid. And so there are bound to be times when one or two of those very many, very unlikely, misfortunes will actually happen to us.

For example, when I fly in an aeroplane, I know that I am taking a (very small) risk. If the plane does crash I am going to call this bad luck rather than search around for some failure of awareness, judgement or action on my part.

Quite probably we will be shocked, hurt, angry, upset and questioning about our bad luck. Quite probably it will be useful for us to re-examine our behaviour, motives and history to try to see if this was not so much bad luck as bad judgement. Sometimes, no doubt, we *will* discover something that we were previously unaware of; so that, with hindsight, we will see that this 'accident' was less of an accident than it first seemed to be.

Quite often with 'misfortune' there is much that can be learned about ourselves. At the very least we might learn how to cope better with misfortune! But I simply do not believe that there is always necessarily a failure of perception or judgement involved when things go wrong. Sometimes, surely, it really *is* just what it seems to be; bad luck! And there may be no other meaning, nor 'justice' nor 'intention' behind it (Divine or otherwise).

It is immature to talk too much of 'bad luck' when what we really need to do is take good note of where *we* failed. Equally important; I think it is immature to refuse to talk of 'luck' at all. When someone tries to abolish luck then they either take on an 'Atlas Complex', shouldering the weight of the world upon their shoulders, and feeling guilty when they can't get everything to go their way; or else they look upon Nature as a sort of 'Big Daddy' that is holding us by the hand every step of the way.

This latter viewpoint tends to presuppose that everything is 'for the best', everything is ultimately 'fair' and a wonderful learning experience! We may be wise to *act as though* we can learn from everything that happens; such a positive attitude really can help us to cope. If we can make the best of everything without sulking or bitterness, we are much more able to deal with adversity and even find some joy in the toughest circumstances.

However, it is one thing (wisely and genuinely) to make the best of everything. It is quite another (foolishly) to pretend that everything really is for the best! There is simply no evidence for this! On the contrary! And

I think that to pretend that life is more warm, chummy, loving and harmonious than it really is involves a lack of faith and courage; a lack of willingness to find joy in life *despite* its tragedies! Of course it would be easy to be joyful if we could kid ourselves that everything is always wonderful despite appearances. But this involves living in an idealistic and idealised life-of-our-dreams rather than in the real world, with its real ecstacies and its equally real sorrows!

As Dale Carnegie (the classic self-help writer of the 1940s) used to say: "If Fate hands you a lemon, see if you can turn it into a lemonade!"

... Good and sensible stuff; but you'll spoil it if you believe either that you will always succeed or that underneath all the nasty appearances there are really no lemons at all! Sometimes, I am sure, things are rough, tough, cruel, destructive and unfair not just 'on the surface', but 'underneath' as well! Reality can be both nicer and nastier than appearances. O.K. so the capacity for good and virtue is always there in us all; but often it may seem next-to-impossible to know how to release it. The capacity for evil and viciousness is just as real and ever-present; and never let us pretend that we have 'just about' got rid of one or the other, or that we always know for sure where each of these lie. The dance or embrace that good and evil has with its opposite is in many respects mysterious in the extreme and it cannot be finally and neatly unravelled here or anywhere else.

In many people's story books everything always turns out for the best in the end. But that is just in the story books! It *may* sometimes happen in real life. But not necessarily or always so. This can be vexing, dispiriting, inspiring, exciting and much besides. It's up to us – to some extent!

54. I need to be more **honest**.

We may say that Truth is a virtue; yet we often find that some dishonesty is easier and more congenial for us – at least in the short run. Our dishonesty may not be gross or blatant; more often it is subtle, slight or hidden... As we mature, we grow cunning, sophisticated and devious; and this means that we only rarely feel the need to tell big, black, gross lies; instead we take a 'softly-softly' approach. For example:

We say much that *is* true; but we don't tell the *whole* truth; or we describe the truth in such a way that (we know) the other person won't hear it; or we talk about something else altogether. We evade, distract, ignore, massage, manipulate, bend and burnish the truth so that the appearance is not the same as the reality. In 1,001 ways we manage, if we are skilled enough, to avoid being honest without actually telling any lies! Or, even more skilled, we succeed in being honest without actually telling the truth! Or, most skilled of all, we tell the truth in such a way, and in such circumstances, with such intentions, that it ends up in being a lie! These skills are by no means restricted to politicians.

'Honesty is the best policy' – as the old saying goes; and it is probably true in the longer run if we can bear to face it. But even in our attempts to be more honest we can run into difficulties.

Much of the trouble can arise because, when we embark on a policy of greater honesty, we will often find that we will tell *more* of the truth but still not the *whole* truth and *nothing but* the truth. And so these extra bits of (partial) 'truth' can have highly destructive and distorting consequences, so that the outcome is still vicious and we are still being essentially 'inauthentic'.

An obvious example of this can be found in many interpersonal relationships. One person may decide "I'm going to be more honest from now on with Jim (or Joan)". Truth, they decide, is a virtue, and if the relationship is to be more 'real' it will have to be more honest. And so they launch into a declaration of all the resentments and irritations – petty or otherwise – that have bothered them about this other person (or these people) for the past (however many) years. All the cobwebs must be blown away; the dirty washing must be displayed; there must be a clear sweep; a cleaning of the decks, a new searing, open, searching honest examination of "what is really happening".

All too often the other person cannot cope with this sudden attack; (s)he feels badly hurt and may well decide to counter-attack with a great onslaught of candid 'honesty' of his or her own. Both parties then begin to feel badly hurt, the relationship gets damaged and the whole process can end up with bitterness, ill-will and a lack of trust on all sides.

How can this be? If honesty is the best policy, how can it so easily turn into such a disaster? The truth, I suggest, is that if we are to be truly honest and really get a full picture of what is going on then we need to look not just at the content of what we are saying, but also at the intentions that we may have when we make our proclamations of 'honesty'. Furthermore, we need to look at the effects on others of what we are saying, and we need to be aware of the way in which what we say is, or might be, perceived and interpreted by our listeners.

If you are to have real honesty in communication it is not enough just to look at the message. You have also got to look at the intention, the context and the reception that this message is likely to produce. And so, for example, I might decide that what I have to say about another person really is the honest truth (as I see it). But what if I discover that my underlying intention in telling this part of the truth is in many ways *spiteful*? Or that it is likely to undermine and damage the other person? Or that it is likely to be perceived and interpreted as vicious regardless of whether or not it is so. Or that, although it is true, it will detract from and interfere with other things that are truly and more usefully and honestly going on between us at the time?

Honesty is a virtue, but, like all the other virtues, the practice of putting it into effect can often require a great deal of skill, a sense of what is appropriate to the occasion, a wider view of how this particular interaction will fit into a larger context of where we are with each other and where we are trying to go. There is no use in pretending that this is simple. It often is *not* simple and we are bound to make lots of mistakes if we are to learn at all.

Often, indeed, the virtue of honesty will appear to conflict with other virtues; like tact, respect, good-will, intelligence, sensitivity, good timing, and a sense of priority and proportion. None of this means that we need to sell ourselves out in relation to 'the truth', but it does mean that, in engaging with larger

Truths, we often need to keep smaller statements of 'honesty' in their proper place! In other words, just as there are too many 'politicians' and not enough 'statesmen' in the wider society, so we need to be more statesmanlike in handling our own lives.

Needless to say, such fine-sounding phrases can easily be, and often are, co-opted by cynics and used to rationalise their own selfish and amoral manoeuverings. That is the way of it, and it is often very difficult to know if we are surveying 'the Truth' from a genuinely lofty perch, or from what is in fact a low, narrow and foggy ledge!

"I am honest
Thou art tactless
He is cruel and vicious"

... Summarises our tendency to consider ourselves to be good judges of honesty, while seeing others as lacking judgement and the ability to take account of the wider context.

I myself have been a part of the encounter group sub-culture of the 1960s and 70s that, in reacting to what it saw as the bad faith, dishonesty, image-making and wheeler-dealing of so much of society, attached great importance to 'honesty', openness and intimacy. Initially, it all seemed so simple! With courage, faith and hope we could throw off our self-imposed chains of dishonest dealing and face a 'New Dawn' where everyone was 'real', 'authentic', 'straight', 'up-front', 'right there', 'genuine' etc.

What I have discovered is that, the more I learn about honesty and other aspects of human communication, the more difficult it seems to be to balance all the various principles at stake in, for example, reconciling honesty with tact. I have not abandoned the principle of honesty as the best policy (my *practice* of course has always lagged far behind). But I see that it is often very difficult to know when my (inevitably partial) 'truth' is likely to obstruct or distort my attempts to 'get through to' others.

I think the Encounter group, 'flower-power', New Age, 'New Dawn' people often made another, related, mistake. They were (and are) most unhappy about the cool, detached, distant, overly-formal, dishonest, inauthentic 'role playing' style of conventional society; and want to replace this with a world where people are more straight, real, authentic, genuine, open and 'upfront'. This is all very well, but the danger is that we can make the mistake of believing that to be 'real' with someone involves being intimate with them and (somewhat crudely) direct and simple in our dealings with them.

Over and over again, I have come across people (from these sub-cultures) who, in order to prove how real and genuine they are, have attempted to be more open and intimate than they have (genuinely) wanted or needed to be. The consequence is that their relationships take on an essentially phony pseudo-intimacy that takes everyone further and further away from the truth of what is going on.

If I am to be (genuinely) real, honest and authentic I need to find the different levels of openness and intimacy that seem appropriate with the different people I meet. I cannot conceivably be intimate and open with everyone. Even if I wanted to (and I don't) there isn't time; and nobody really wants to be burdened with a running commentary from others about their every thought, feeling, conflict and desire. In any case, such private experiences run faster than our ability to describe them. Therefore we have to be selective about how much we share of ourselves with others. We are only aware of a small part of any 'truth', and we can only describe a small part of that!

55. I need to **relax**.

Our ability to relax is inextricably connected to the ways in which we deal with worry, guilt and (have you thought of this one?) – ambition. All of these come in useful, less useful and useless varieties and it is most important that we learn to distinguish one from another. We have dealt with guilt elsewhere (see section twenty-five); let us begin here with the subject of worry.

This, as I say, can come in different varieties; and we need to establish which category we are dealing with. Worry is useful if, as a result of 'worrying' about the problem, we are likely to learn from and make a better job of it. It is less useful if we have already worried enough about the matter, and would be making better use of our time if we were doing something else. Worry is useless if the worrying stops us from effectively tackling the problem and also prevents us from doing anything else as well. In this way, worry can become painfully paralysing.

Useful worry (some people wouldn't want to call this worry at all) involves learning from past mistakes and constructively anticipating future difficulties so that, when the actual situation confronts us, we are more likely to deal with it effectively. Worry of the useless variety, on the other hand, generally consists in our indulging in endless destructive fantasies of future catastrophes; taking the form – "What if...?" It also involves pointless regrets about the past; of the form; "If only...!" Such destructive worry is closely inter-related with tension and relaxation, since the more we are uselessly worrying the more we are likely to be getting uselessly tense.

Useless worries, fears and fantasies produce useless body tension – as we brace ourselves against a danger that presently exists only in our mind! Such tension, like the worry that stimulates it, serves no purpose; but merely distracts, paralyses and exhausts us. It can even make us ill!

It is well worth exploring in some detail the ways we excessively and uselessly make ourselves tense. We need to see what effects all this is having on our body and become more aware of the particular muscles that we are holding too rigidly. Useless tension can have very damaging effects, and, in order to deal with it, we need to be aware of the way we needlessly screw ourselves up to deal with imaginary threats.

The danger in this is that, in the very process of becoming more aware of our tension, we start to worry and get tense about being tense! Obviously this is no help at all. There are many physical approaches to relaxation and many books, tapes and training programmes available. (For example, see 'Suggested Reading' page 212.) I simply cannot do justice to this vast subject in the space available, and I think that it is wiser not to try!

Physical tension is fine when it is the muscle tension needed to take constructive action. Without some tension in certain key muscles, for example, I would not be able to stand, sit or walk; but would simply fall over in a (relaxed) heap on the floor! However, there are few tasks that require a great deal of tension in my jaw, forehead, shoulders or fists. Quite commonly, though, people tense up these muscles to 'assist' them in doing whatever it is that they are trying (oh so hard!) to do.

The first step in dealing with destructive varieties of worry and tension is to become more aware of them and to see them in all their uselessness. It does not generally require a great deal of thought or analysis to determine whether or not our worry and tension is serving a useful purpose. For example, once we are aware that we go in for a great deal of jaw tightening or shoulder tension or deep frowning, it does not require much insight to see that these behaviours, far from helping us, are a pain and a hindrance.

There is no point in my saying to myself, "I must stop worrying, I must stop worrying". This will just serve to make me feel even more worried! Similarly, if I go on and on saying, "I mustn't think about this; I mustn't think about this" then the very act of saying (or thinking) "I mustn't think this" will in itself ensure that you go on thinking it! In your attempt to not think of something, you have to form in your mind an image of the very thing you are trying not to think about. In other words, you have to think of it!

Instead, the best move is to substitute the useless worry with more constructive, pleasurable or rewarding thoughts or actions. And *when* (not if) we find ourselves slipping back into useless worry once again, we can gently but firmly take ourselves back to what we would most prefer to do (or most value doing). After practising this for a few tens of thousands of times, we start to learn how to avoid useless worry; but it is quite unrealistic to think that we will ever be able to abolish it!

Similarly with useless tension. We can ask, "Does the tension (and the *amount* of tension) in this muscle help or hinder me in doing what I'm trying to do right now?" The answer will almost always be obvious once we have become aware of the degree of tension that exists. There are many ways of dealing with useless muscle tension. (See reading list, page 212.)

Relaxation, ideally, is not something that we try to do for half an hour or so *after* we have finished all the work, chores, social engagements etc. Better to take a more relaxed approach to everything that we do, so that we manage to be as relaxed as possible even when (or particularly when) we are busy. This does not mean that we get less done. On the contrary, we will manage to do more since, with a smoother, calmer, more graceful approach to what we do, we will make fewer mistakes and waste less energy.

So often we rush around and get ourselves much too tense. We exhaust ourselves and become very inefficient. If we were to slow down and calm down a little, we could become far more productive and competent. Worse yet, our 'busyness' prevents us from keeping a proper perspective on what we are doing, so that we get lost in one distraction after another. We then fail to see the wood from the trees, which leads to still more error and waste.

Some people can learn to relax simply by paying more attention to their body and what they are doing with it; and by trying out one or another of the many physical approaches to relaxation. For some people a calming of their body will lead to a calming of the mind. Others need, or prefer, to approach the subject from the other direction and thus calm the body as a result of first seeking to calm the mind. (After all, the activity of each is both cause and effect of the other.)

The root of the trouble may be that you are excessively ambitious about what you think you 'should' be achieving – both with the short- and the long-term goals you have set yourself. You may need to tackle directly these self-defeating attitudes, beliefs and expectations. If we endlessly expect ourselves to be able to become, and to do, far more than we can realistically achieve then we are doomed to a life of self-torture, disappointment and mania. We will be constantly rushing around trying to live up to impossible timetables and impossibly high standards, and we will become chronically tense, anxious and (ultimately) depressed.

It is often very difficult to know whether we are demanding too little or too much of ourselves. If we demand too little then we don't make use of our full potential, and so we miss the real pleasures of self-expression, commitment and self-fulfilment. We may have a quiet, relaxed and peaceful time, relatively free of suffering, tension and unease; but we will have done so as a result of opting out of our lives. This is what I like to call 'serenity-on-the-cheap'.

At the other extreme, if we demand too much of ourselves we will never be able to relax and be at peace. We will never be able to savour life, since we will always be too busy trying to capture, mould, or transform it. And, given our inevitably limited powers, we will always feel disillusioned, disappointed and depressed.

Our happiness and peace of mind are not primarily a consequence of our 'luck' or overall 'talent'. They are much more the result of the gap that we maintain between what we've got and what we want! You may have achieved very little, but if your expectations are even more slight you will nonetheless be quite content. On the other hand, you may have accomplished a very great deal, yet if your desires and expectations are much greater even than your achievements you will remain frustrated and discontented!

The more we get, the more we start to want, and thus our discontent may remain much the same despite the improvements we may have made (or been blessed with). More painful, of course, is the situation where we start to get less and less than we'd ever hoped for, and less than we used to achieve. In this situation our discontent may start to rise dangerously and, if we are to cope at all, it may become essential for us to *reduce* our expectations. Such a retreat, needless to say, is always more difficult to deal with than an advancement of our expectations, desires and achievements.

In other words, there are, if you like, useful and useless varieties of discontent. A certain degree of dissatisfaction is useful since it provides us with the spur to push ourselves a little further and thus express and fulfil ourselves a little more. But too much discontent becomes self-defeating and destructively tension-making. It leads us to feel disillusioned, depressed, dispirited and miserable.As a result of it, we are likely to give up in despair and achieve much less than we would have done were we to have been more realistic. Too much ambition, *and* too little, leads us to waste ourselves and our potential.

56. I am in **conflict** with myself about this problem.

Human thinking is complex because, as well as being able to think, we can *know* that we are thinking, and we can think *about* what we have just thought. Indeed, we can take this further, and think about what we have been thinking about... and so on. In other words, we can be aware of ourselves thinking, and we can assess, judge, evaluate and contradict previous thoughts.

Similarly with our emotions. We can have feelings about something that is going on 'out there' in the world; but we can also have feelings about the emotion that we have just felt! So, for example, we can be angry about something that someone else just did; and then we can get angry about being angry (again) – and thus get still more angry. We can blame the other person. Then we can feel sad that all this is happening. We can feel frustrated or bored about the sequence so far. Then we can feel amusement, and so on and so on – for as long as you want to go on having thoughts and feelings about thoughts and feelings.

To put it another way: not only do we have feelings and thoughts about events in the world around us; we also have feelings and thoughts about our feelings and thoughts. We have meta-thoughts and meta-feelings, if you like; or second, third, fourth and fifth order thoughts and feelings.

This sequence may seem a bit tortuous and, indeed, sometimes the actual experience feels the same! It goes on a very great deal of the time. We may pretend to ourselves and others that we have only just one thought and feeling about a particular object, person or event; so that when someone asks "what do you think (or feel) about...?" we are likely to think that we should give just one answer. But it is far more likely that in fact we could give a dozen answers that describe the contrary and contradictory thoughts and feelings that we may have in just twenty seconds after being asked "What do you think and feel about... (whatever)...?"

Often, our opinions and feelings are not fixed and static. They shift and change. We think one thing and then its opposite. We take one view, and then another, and then another. We have the brains to see the subtlety and complexity of many questions, and so we can turn them over and over, in our minds; looking at them from many different angles, taking a view of them from a great variety of perspectives.

If we take a more simple-minded or simple-hearted approach to problems, people and events, then we will tend to see them in a much more one dimensional way, and think that the single 'key-hole' from which we survey our world is the 'one and only' view that there is. We will then be free of a great deal of inner turmoil and conflict but at the price of having a fixed, naive, unchanging and essentially simplistic view of everything. We will have 'peace of mind' at the expense of having a simple mind. And then we will be able to sit, like the cat, with a simple certainty that all is as it should be – food, fire, carpet – completion!

Fortunately, or unfortunately (depending on how you are feeling about it right now), these simple certainties and calm feelings of assurance that are possibly available to 'lower' species are not so easily experienced by us. We can question, we can doubt, we can argue within ourselves as well as with others; we can send our imagination and questioning far ahead of our knowledge. In this way, we can become acutely conscious of all that we don't know and aren't sure about. (Compare this with the cat; who doesn't know that it doesn't know, and consequently doesn't care about it! It doesn't even wish to ask!)

We as human beings, on the other hand, can query and question everything. We can ask and doubt and argue until our head is spinning; until we are sick, weary, tense and confused. We can get tense, not just about real threats that are right here before us, as any animal needs to, and does, do; we can also get tense about the *thought* of the threats that there *might* be here tomorrow, or next week or next year. And we can then get tense at the thought of all the dangers, risks, problems and demons we faced last week and last year!

This capacity to think and feel about that which is not here before me; ie. to think and feel about my memories and any of my other thoughts and feelings – is what makes us (more or less) unique; on this planet at any rate. It is the source of most of our joys and extraordinary achievements; it is also the source of most of our pains, terrors, turmoils and fears! Used wisely, our brain can help us to feel, see and do far more than any other animal can ever imagine or understand. Used with less wisdom it can, and does, pitch us into a hell of turmoil, conflict and suffering that is, also, far worse than the fantasies or nightmares that any other animal is capable of creating. Even with the wisest possible use, this ability to think and feel about our thoughts and feelings is bound to pitch us regularly into a very great deal of pain and turmoil. Indeed, our capacity to feel great joy probably grows in proportion to our capacity to experience great pain, so that if you successfully deaden yourself to one you will probably damage your ability to experience the other.

When we are in conflict with ourselves we will often experience regular patterns of thought, followed by their contradictory or contrary opposites. It can sometimes seem as though there was an uproarious 'parliament' inside us; or as though a variety of sub-personalities inhabited us.

We might often ask the question – "What do I *really* think?" or (to put it another way) which of these characters inside me is the 'real' me? But this question is misplaced since we really *do* think and feel these contrary and contradictory thoughts and feelings. If we try to attach ourselves to just one of our responses then we will fail to benefit from what the others have to contribute. Worse still, we will exacerbate the conflict inside us, since all those other views will insist all the more on being heard and will go to great lengths to get a hearing. They are just a part of us, and we will create great tension and difficulties for ourselves if we try to 'sit on' ourselves!

One important question remains unanswered though: "If I am quite divided within myself about what I think, feel and want, then how am I supposed to be able to make decisions and take action?" Clearly, if we wait until we are absolutely certain and 'of one mind' about something, we might wait forever before deciding and doing. On those rare occasions when we *are* absolutely certain, and have no doubts, unanswered questions, alternative proposals or opposing feelings at all – then the decision and the action is simple and effortless, and it doesn't even feel like a decision.

The difficulty about decision-making and action, for human beings at least, lies precisely in the fact that we will generally need to decide and act when many parts of ourselves are still questioning and opposing the decision. That is why decisions often seem difficult and actions seem to require a lot of effort.

The effort lies, not in overcoming the problem, but in overcoming our dissident thoughts and feelings about it; for example, our fear, reluctance, resentment, sabotage-attempts, complaints, condemnations, fantasies, contrary and contradictory desires and intentions and our generally wandering mind and heart.

More simple animals don't seem to have so much difficulty with either decisions or action. They rarely think: "I'm not sure what to do here" and they never consider that "this is an enormous effort". They don't conceive of such things since they do not assess, judge, examine, question, doubt or imagine ideal alternatives or potential catastrophes. They just get on with it, and they generally don't have any conception of an alternative to what they are doing. They never think "there must be a better way" or "another" way, and so they don't consider that "this is a terrible/difficult/painful way". If there is pain for them then they wince for as long as the pain lasts, and then, when it has gone, they forget it. (Many of the higher mammals do show signs of being able to reflect just a little on what they are doing; to doubt what they have done and to fear what might happen next. But the difference in these respects between, say, chimpanzees and human beings is, surely, enormous. In any case, the human predicament remains the same regardless of whether or not it is shared by some other species!)

So, then, we often need to decide and act when we are in many ways at odds with ourselves. We need to be strong willed in these circumstances and take action when on balance we judge it to be necessary – even though the 'permanent opposition' is clamouring for us to stop. But exercising a strong will does not mean that we have to try to repress, crush, attack or feel terrible about our other views and voices. They each have a role to play; they each contribute something; they are all part of us and add to the subtlety, complexity and sophistication that we are. And so we can, as it were, thank them, show respect and regard for them, hear them out and, if we judge it necessary, gently and firmly over-rule them. We then take action even though there may still be a clamour inside us – to the effect that (eg.) "it shouldn't be like this; I should be doing something else; I'm scared; what if I fail? why aren't things different? there are too many obstacles; it's too difficult; it's too much trouble" etc.

Often, we will pretend that we are 'of one mind' and that there is not an internal clamour, because we imagine that there is something wrong with us to be so divided within. Others seem to be clear, calm and certain, because *they*, like us, are so often pretending that they are more clear, coherent and consistent than they really are! And so we imagine that we, too, ought to be like this. We then pretend that we really *are*; and we punish ourselves and feel badly about ourselves when we (re)discover that we are not this paragon of chronic consistency.

All could be so much more simple if we could be at peace within this clamouring; trusting the internal conflict, and trusting that, like all the musical instruments playing in a symphony, we can find the underlying harmony in all of this that does not identify with any one voice, but which trusts, and makes good use of, them all. If the conductor of an orchestra were to say, "there are so many different instruments here, which is the real one? Which one is the right one? Which one should be allowed to play all the time?"... then we would recognise that he was fundamentally ignorant about the nature of orchestral music; and that any piece he managed to conduct would be narrow and thin and liable to interruption from all the other irate orchestral players!

Similarly, we too might find far deeper harmonies and much richer insights into ourselves and our world if we could seek to give all our contrary visions and voices a part to play in our overall perception or song. Our various 'voices', or sub-personalities need to be controlled or else we would indulge some at the expense of others. But real control is not of the vicious, repressive sort, but manages to be gentle, tolerant, forgiving and understanding, as well as firm. This reminds me of a saying I came across (I've forgotten where) which struck me as being of fundamental importance:

> The greatest obstacle to 'progress'
> Is the belief that there are some people
> Who are an obstacle to progress.

Similarly, I would suggest:

> The greatest obstacle to one's own 'progress'
> Is the belief that there are some thoughts, feelings, wishes,
> 'parts' of ourselves

That are an obstacle to our own progress.

We can 'hear out' and learn from everything; and, even when we make mistakes, we can learn from and become renewed and empowered by these rather than allowing them to sink us. The bigger and more catastrophic the mistake, and our consequent regret, the deeper and greater is the message available for us to learn, if we will but face it, value it, learn from it.

In the way of the orchestral conductor, if we act wisely, we can manage neither to exclude nor identify with our different voices, opinions, feelings and desires. They each have something to offer us so that we do not need to bury them. But neither do we need to indulge them, get carried away with them, or become bogged down or enmeshed in them. For if we do we will lose perspective, lose sight of all that is available to us; lose our balance. (Although, even in the process of losing it, the lack of balance itself acts as a pointer to where a better perspective might be, so that it too can be used positively.)

The mistake that we can make in all this, though, is to imagine that the balanced, poised, global, 'whole person' viewpoint is somehow always exactly 'in the middle', and always calm and unruffled and somehow entirely free from all tempestuous and painful feelings. Nothing could be further from the truth. Again, the analogy with the orchestral conductor will serve to make this clear.

The conductor, as he brings out each instrument and player, will 'empathise' closely with each particular part. His body will tense with the dramatic chords and loud fanfares; it will relax and flow with the more peaceful and melodious sections and instruments. In other words, the conductor, in 'getting fully involved' with the piece as a whole, will do this by being closely involved with each part in particular. He will not sit detached and unruffled at the back of the auditorium, passively hearing the whole performance; neither will he get so tied up with the drums (say) that he carries on beckoning them to play when he knows that their part is done!

We too can operate along these lines in our own lives, and trust that there can be a harmony *within* our conflicts. We don't find harmony by endlessly sitting beyond or above each conflicting detail of our lives, as some insipid accounts of 'spirituality' suggest. But none of this is easy to put into practice, and only by getting it 'wrong' for much of the time do we start to get an inkling of some of the ways in which we may be more nearly 'right'.

The conductor and players in an orchestra have to practise a great deal before there is much sign of skillful means at work; and our own 'play' is even more difficult to perform because, unlike the conductor, we are much less sure about where all the pieces might be and what should be the tune. Moreover, our 'players' (or sub-personalities if you like) tend to be an undisciplined lot who are often reluctant to co-operate, and who each want to hog the show for themselves!

Nonetheless, for all that it is difficult, the challenge can be seen as a stimulating, invigorating, life enhancing experience, and we can at least begin to see how far we can put some of these principles into practice. It doesn't happen overnight!

57. I feel **stuck** with this problem; and I don't see a way forward.

You can't always avoid feeling stuck. You can't always feel that you're 'on the move' and 'getting somewhere' with your problems. You may prefer this, but don't *expect* it. It's simply unrealistic. And so, quite often, there is nothing that needs to be done about feeling stuck. You simply need to feel it. Then, at least, you can avoid feeling stuck *about* feeling stuck! (You may even learn from the feelings!)

Maybe you are stuck because you are trying too hard? Are you rather frantically tensing up and dashing and scrambling at the problem? Are you willing to be at peace with your 'stuckness' and confusion? If not, then you may be getting into a bit of a 'clinch' and a panic with yourself. Maybe you are 'sitting on' other feelings: like fear, doubt, hostility, confusion... or whatever?

What might happen if you allowed yourself to open up to your feeling of 'stuckness'? Perhaps you fear that the feeling would engulf you? But perhaps it would be more likely to teach you something useful about the problem you are facing? Perhaps you know this already, but you fear that what you must learn might be painful and unpleasant? Maybe it *will* be unpleasant? Maybe you would therefore rather stay stuck?

On the other hand, maybe you are not stuck at all, however much you may feel that you are? Maybe you would rather feel stuck than face up to the fact that you are not? Maybe the alternatives seem too painful? We sometimes put ourselves into our seemingly 'stuck' position because it seems like the best (or least worst) that we can find. It may, of course, be hard for us to admit to this! Do you want to stay stuck or would you prefer to see if it might be better to try to 'unstick' yourself?

We often choose to be 'stuck' since it frequently looks like the safest option at least in the short run; especially when we're scared of the (often risky and uncertain) alternatives. Guilt then arises as a result of our shame at allowing fear to get on top of us. It may have a role to play here, but it is of no use if we flagellate ourselves!

Do you feel stuck because you feel helpless, out of control, passive and not responsible for what is happening? Do you feel dwarfed by the larger events happening around you? Do you wish you had more power? Are you at least making full use of the power that you *do* have?

We can feel very tired, stuck, jaded, powerless and hopeless when we don't at least 'play the cards' or use the powers that we *do* have. We can, and do, complain that events are larger than we are, and that we seem relatively insignificant. But the complainers are generally only using, perhaps, ten per cent of themselves; the rest of their potential is hidden away even from themselves; or they keep it stored up in reserve for when they 'really' might need it, or for the day when they, others, and the world as a whole deserve their full commitment!

On the other hand, those who, after due forethought, really *are* prepared to make a leap, take a plunge, or 'have a go', will find that they are now using themselves more fully, and making better use of whatever they have. Such people tend to feel much less stuck, much more satisfied with, and at peace with, themselves; and much more able to come to terms with the inevitable limits and constraints that we all face. For at least these latter people can say – "Well, I tried. I've lived. I've set myself goals and attempted to achieve them. I may have failed many times, but at least I was willing to have a go. I don't feel that I'm 'wasting' or 'wasted' of myself and my time." As the old saying goes:

Better to have loved and lost
than never have loved at all.

... and we can, additionally, amend this to:

Better to have lived and lost
than never to have lived at all.

If we won't allow ourselves to feel stuck from time to time but instead, run away from these feelings, then we are likely to find that we will actually *be* stuck! After all, let's remember, the very fact that you are feeling stuck itself shows that you are, in a very important sense, actually 'on the move' inside.

The feelings of stuckness come – not when we are entirely accepting the situation we are in but when we are fighting against it; when what we want is some way ahead of what we are getting. And so we may not be 'on the move' in the actual world, but we are certainly on the move in our intentions, plans, preferences, goals, yearnings and ideals. And, however painful an experience this may be, it is in fact very often a necessary first step towards making the changes we want to make in the actual world. If our visions never ran ahead of reality; if we never yearned for more than we have; if we never felt constrained nor 'stuck' by our circumstances, then this would generally indicate, not that we were really using ourselves to the full but, rather, that we were not really pushing ourselves very much and instead rather idling along in our lives.

We can get all we want if we are simply prepared to want all we get, without pushing ourselves at all. But, this way, we won't do as much as we might otherwise have done. Such passive acceptance may give us a more tranquil time; but it will be the tranquility of the backwater, the comfortable stupor of the person who hides on the edge of life; who 'hides his own light under a bushel'.

So, then, those people who have really managed to 'move' themselves have (unless they have been very fortunate) generally been the ones who have been willing to feel stuck, feel constrained, hemmed in, and who have been willing to 'chafe at the bit' at times and pull hard.

58. I **don't tolerate** 'setbacks' very well; I like everything to fit my plans.

At one extreme, there are individuals (and whole societies) who make life a misery for themselves and others because they are never satisfied, and always chasing around for more. Such people seem to think that the whole of life is a great preparation and rehearsal for when 'perfection' has been achieved. Only then, they believe, could they ever sit back and enjoy it. And so, because they are always living 'for tomorrow' (and tomorrow never comes) they never really get to live at all; but instead go on making their feverish preparations and arrangements, in a rush, rush, rush!

At the other extreme are those (individuals and cultures) that are basically too accepting of life as it is. Never mind injustice, oppression, starvation, inhumanity. Never mind that there may be a 'better widgit' that we could make to do this job and better ways of thinking and acting; new mysteries to unravel. "Let us just accept and allow everything to be as it is. We enjoy the moment as it is. Go with 'the flow'. Be with what is. Nature is wonderful and no man-made thing can compete with it. All will be provided. Relax! See the 'Golden Vision' within."

This is all very well. The person 'lives in the present' and relaxes and smiles (rather smugly and inanely perhaps). But he becomes fatalistic. He doesn't use the powers that he has. In giving up all suffering that arises from our unfulfilled dreams and lost attachments, he gives up much of his personality and much joy besides. He tolerates and 'allows' all kinds of mess that we could have otherwise cleaned up to the benefit of all. He *stays* stuck even though he doesn't *feel* stuck! He lives like a cat or a cabbage, and thus fails to use his individual human powers. Moreover, in refusing to go near specifically human misery he fails to realise the uniquely human joys of achieving complex goals.

How then, are we to achieve a balance between demanding too much and asking too little of ourselves and our world? As ever, it isn't easy. There isn't a formula, nor an objective and absolute criterion with which everyone can agree. We have to judge it for ourselves and expect to get it wrong quite regularly in order to discover some of the ways in which it might be 'right'. It is unlikely that we will ever all agree about it; yet everything that we, and others, ever do can serve to help us unravel this mystery just a little more.

Within our turmoil, confusion, questioning, doubt, uncertainty, striving and struggling we can find a much deeper harmony than the shallow tranquillity of a 'world that fits our plans', or a 'world devoid of plans'.

If we are really to be accepting and at peace, we need to accept that, as humans, we tend to strive and struggle to 'somewhere, we know not where'; and that this is a part of the Human Condition. We can only find peace and stay human if we are prepared to be at peace with, and within, our turmoil, ignorance, confusion, struggle and conflict. We need to trust all this and learn from it without destroying ourselves in the process through excessive zeal or bitterness; and without running away from human trials and tragedies by retreating into fatalism. None of this is easy; it is much easier to run to one, or the other, extreme position; to polarise; to dig in to one position or another.

Presently, many Western cultures seem to embody the one extreme of obsessive striving; while Eastern cultures go to the other extreme of embracing an apathetic fatalism. However, this is changing. Each style of being-in-the-world can learn from the other, and there are signs that this is beginning to happen. Don't, however, expect some fixed or final synthesis.

59. I see this problem as a terrible **burden** and **obstacle** in my life. I feel as though I have been hit by this problem.

Are you the sort of person who is always immersed in the minutiae of your life, without ever stepping back and taking an overall view of what you are about? Do you see 'the trees' but not 'the wood' as a whole? If so, does this sometimes get you into difficulties? What sort of problems arise from taking such a short-term view?

On the other hand, maybe this is not your problem. Maybe you go to the other extreme and spend most of the time trying to survey everything from a great height; without ever getting closely involved and committed to the day-to-day details? If so, what price do you pay?

We cannot expect to know very much about the world we inhabit if we only ever survey it, in our imagination, from 10,000 feet above ground, or if we only ever stare closely at one small corner of our life. We need to take *both* the broad perspective *and* be willing to get in close as well; to shuttle backwards and forwards from the general to the particular as appropriate, so that each informs and helps to make sense of the other.

The excessively theoretical, philosophical individual is so anxious to preserve the larger picture, principle or spirit of the exercise that he fails to engage sufficiently in the particular. Consequently, his abstractions and generalisations become like 'castles in the clouds' (or, if you prefer, 'castles in the sand'). Either way, they have no firm root in everyday reality. They become armchair speculations; empty, useless and meaningless.

In trying to discover the spirit and meaning of life, such an excessive generaliser ends up by, in effect, refusing to play the game at all. Instead, he becomes a voyeur of life. Any tranquility or (appearance of) wisdom he achieves is really a torpor, an anaesthetic. Such a person may imagine that he is gazing down on 'reality as a whole', on his own excessively abstract fantasy. He may beam with delight at his own breakthroughs into 'the Truth'; but his detachment and serenity are cheap copies of the real thing; like that of the drug-induced junkie's attachment to his own delusion.

Meaning and insight cannot come simply from endless speculation, observation, generalisation and introspection. We do not become enlightened merely by gazing at our own navels or reading abstract philosophy (or self-help manuals!). We need in addition (and more crucially) to take *action*, to make commitments, to take risks, to become fully *involved* in our own particular small corner of the world.

It is important to take a perspective on our problems; to get a larger view on all those day-to-day details. On the other hand, we can't expect to achieve this perspective if we've never allowed ourselves in the first place to be fully involved with and committed to all the day-to-day detail. After all, how can we step back if we've never stepped forward into that daily morass? How can we make some kind of advance on what we are doing if we always want to go into retreat? How can we put our smaller views into a larger perspective if we're never prepared to engage with these smaller perspectives and actions? We may want to try to put the whole jig-saw of our lives together into a pattern that makes sense to us; but to do this we have to be prepared to be fully involved with each piece at a time, for much of the time.

What does it feel like, though, when you are 'down on the ground' rather than 'up in the clouds looking down'? From this day-to-day perspective, does it feel as though problems *ambush* you, or hit you, or block your path, or weigh you down? Do you feel that you have to 'get over' them, 'get round' them or 'get them off your back'? When you succeed do you feel joy and exhilaration? Do you feel better, lighter, happier? And when you fail, do you feel still more burdened, more blocked, more injured, in pain and 'put out' by these problems?

People often experience problems in this way; and, if you do too, it is easy for you mistakenly to conclude that life would be wonderful if you could only get rid of all the problems! In other words, you can start to believe that problems, far from being very much part of the process of our living our lives, are a snag, an obstacle and burden that *prevents* us from living. We then imagine that life would be fine, wonderful, happy – that we could really live it to the full – if we never had any problems at all.

This, though, is complete fantasy. If, by some miracle, you only ever had a few simple problems to tackle; with everything more or less exactly fitting in with your plans, you would not be blissfully happy for long. Instead, you would feel bored, listless, under-employed, un-stretched, tired, unstimulated, lost and without a sense of meaning and purpose. You would, in fact, soon find that this seemingly 'problem-free' existence was beginning to become a major problem in its own right!

You would then have (perhaps you *do* have?) a new, and very considerable problem to face (and one that is presently experienced by many people): the problem of being bored, not having enough to do, not being sufficiently challenged. This problem can also, in some respects, provide its own solution. After all, if you are really prepared to face up to and learn from your feelings of boredom and listlessness it soon becomes exciting, unpredictable, painful and uncertain; and not at all dead, flat or empty! Rather than feeling empty, you are full of boredom. In other words, emptiness, like every other feeling, can be a very 'full', fertile and fulfilling experience; *if* we are prepared to face it. Such feelings, although unpleasant, serve as useful pointers to help you to see what action you need to take next.

If we are faced with too many very tough problems, then we need to see and to act with wisdom in order to avoid being needlessly damaged by them. Similarly, to be faced with too *few* problems can be a major challenge.

60. I feel that I am constantly **struggling** and **battling** with my problems.

Do you experience problems as a struggle, battle or conflict? Do you think of yourself as having victories, defeats, successes and failures in relation to problems? It can sometimes be of use for us to look upon problems in this rather militaristic manner. Such a perception can galvanise us into action, get the adrenaline flowing, wake us up and help us to 'pull ourselves together' so that we make renewed efforts.

But can you see the limits, dangers and illusions of this sort of militaristic thinking? Problems, after all, do not try to beat us, outwit us, surprise, undermine, attack, overwhelm or do anything else to us. After all, they are not living, conscious entities with intentions, plans, motives and feelings of their own! Do you sometimes imagine that they are alive and malevolent in this way?

We can solve, or cope with a problem, but we cannot beat it, any more than it can beat us! We can make progress in our understanding of the problem; but we can't overwhelm it. Conversely, we can't be overwhelmed by it even though we may feel exhausted, frustrated (or whatever else) in the process of trying to tackle or come to terms with a problem.

In other words, the kind of militaristic analogies we often use are just that – analogies. We think of our tussles with problems as though they were battles; but the danger is that we start to think we really are involved in a battle.

It *is* possible for us to change the way we think and feel about problems; and change the way we apprehend and experience them. Such changes are not easy, because it is difficult to change old habitual beliefs and attitudes, and (perhaps) impossible to do so 'overnight'.

Our habitual way of seeing problems is generally in terms of battle, struggle, victory, defeat, success, failure and all the rest. But other analogies and comparisons are probably even more useful. For example, problems can also be seen as something that you *dance* with, co-operate and 'flow' with. And even when you see yourself struggling in a tense way with them you can, if you choose, relax about feeling tense (rather than getting tense about feeling tense). We can feel co-operative, tentative and exploratory about the (imagined) struggle, rather than struggling with it!

Similarly, instead of winning or losing in relation to problems, we can look upon them as mysteries to be unravelled; involving exploration, adventure, discovery, risk and *surprise*! Words like victory and defeat do not objectively describe the process of problem-solving; they merely reveal our own self-appraisal of what we have done; and the gap between our expectations and our achievements.

Of course, we all have preferences; and I would not prefer it to be otherwise! But, if we can't get what we would *prefer* to get, we don't have to see this as a 'catastrophe', or 'failure', or 'deeply wounding' experience. Indeed, a preference is something that we might, more wisely and mildly, prefer rather than insist upon!

When we operate with problems in this more tentative, exploratory fashion we can find that there is no longer so much of a battle to be fought or territory to be 'won'; but simply, and more usefully, an adventure to be experienced. Even if we continue to see things in terms of battle, struggle and all the rest we can still have an adventure about this experience!

61. I am **trying too hard** with this problem.

We know, well enough, what is going on when we are *not trying* hard enough...

We let our attention wander.

We don't face up to and over-rule our fears, distractions and delaying tactics.

We allow ourselves to lose perspective.

We let short-term conflict triumph over longer-term well-being; and

We refuse to face up to and go through a certain amount of inevitable discomfort, uncertainty, confusion, doubt, and conflict.

This is all familiar enough.

But what is it to *try too hard* in relation to a problem? In some ways it is the opposite of the above list: ie ...

* We don't let our attention wander enough in ways that would be fertile, creative and useful to us.

* We ruthlessly try to over-ride and over-rule all our fears,

fantasy, distraction and delaying tactics; and consequently we fail to see that (sometimes) all these have something constructive to offer us.

* In our efforts to hold and keep a perspective we attempt to form one prematurely, and thus we lose contact with the nuts and bolts of the problem.

* We puritanically force ourselves towards what we see as the long term goal, and thus lose sight of some of the virtues and values of flexibility, surprise, comfort and rest.

* We battle so hard to overcome our uncertainty, confusion, doubt and conflict that we fail to see that often these have much to offer us – and frequently, in any case, they are inevitable.

* We try to be more clear and in control than is presently realistic or possible, and in this way we actually lose some of our clarity and control.

If we sometimes tried *less* hard we would find that many insights, useful experiences, guides, clues, hints and answers just come to us when we just relax a little, and let ourselves be a little more patient, open, receptive and intuitive.

There are times when we don't try hard enough and lazily imagine that 'something will turn up if I just wait for it'. But, sometimes, it is a mistake to try and try and try again. On occasions we need to be a little more passive, receptive, tentative, open, still, tranquil and ready to receive whatever comes along – from inside or outside of us, and without pretending that we are able to always know in advance how this strategy might work.

If we were just a little more receptive in this way, we would know more often when to wait quietly for inspiration to come along, and when to actively and energetically go after it!

One way of 'trying too hard' is that of trying to rehearse everything we do in advance. Rehearsal has its place, but if we do too much of this there will be no time for us to move on to the actual 'performance'. We will become perfectionistic, and the very process of rehearsal, self-monitoring and review will interfere with our actual performance.

Do you over-rehearse when you are trying to talk to someone? It can be useful, up to a point, to try and figure out what you want to say before you say it! But some people try too hard in this respect and try to 'say' or 'see' perfectly clear sentences in their minds before they actually say them out loud. It then becomes virtually impossible for them to speak at all. They become tongue-tied, because by the time they have got their sentence planned the conversation has moved on.

You cannot say one thing while at the same time checking out what you are going to say in ten seconds time. If you try, you will have to keep on stopping to work out exactly what you are going to say next! This means that everything you say will be terribly halting and hesitant. You will also sound rather 'flat', since your words will not be alive and spontaneous; you will in fact be repeating out loud something that you have just said in your head – and so your words will have a rather dead and 'second-hand' quality about them.

By trying too hard to rehearse your words you can get yourself into a vicious spiral. Your performance becomes clumsy and halting and you quickly sense that you are making a bit of a mess of what you are doing. Consequently you try even harder, rehearse even more carefully, and thus paralyse yourself even more successfully! As a result of checking everything you are saying, you will prevent yourself from talking at all. You will dry up completely!

If you are to speak (or write) in a way that is immediate and authentic, you quite often have to discover what you are saying only after you have said it. You may then want to amend, qualify or withdraw your words, or reject them altogether. But you will make more progress in all these respects if you avoid rehearsing everything in your head first. This means that you must take risks and be willing to make mistakes. Only then can you achieve the maximum (possible) degree of control of what you are doing.

You will lose control if you don't try hard enough; if you refuse to make plans, refuse to review your performance and fail to monitor what you are doing. Too much spontaneity will make you careless, slip-shod and prone to (unnecessary) error.

Equally, you will also lose control if you go to the other extreme and try too hard. An obsession with plans, reviews, self-awareness and self-control will (paradoxically) take you further and further away from effective self-control! A refusal to take risks and make mistakes will maximise rather than minimise the number of mistakes you make!

62. I am making more mistakes than I need to because I am **not sufficiently aware** of what I am doing.

Do you sometimes find that, as a result of not paying attention, you go into a kind of daze or trance? Do you sometimes sink into a kind of stupor of doziness and inattention? Are you necessarily more aware and awake in the daytime when your eyes are open? There are probably degrees of wakefulness; and we can be as out of contact with the world in our day-dreams as we are when we dream at night.

It is very easy to slip into regular patterns of behaviour that we never re-examine or reassess. Such habits can initially provide a constructive and labour-saving routine that gives shape, structure and direction to our lives. But, if we never re-examine these habits, they can become less and less useful and relevant, and we end up trapped in a rut rather than supported by a framework. Consequently, we fail to see or make use of other, more effective, ways of approaching our problems.

When we were very young, we tended to look around and within ourselves with bright eyes and a genuine curiosity and wish to learn. There was so much mystery and excitement, and we threw ourselves into what we did with energy and enthusiasm. But as we get older (and this aging process can sometimes occur terrifyingly early) our attention may become duller and more sluggish. We may not look, or listen, or smell, or taste, or touch, or feel because 'I already know', or 'I don't want to know' or 'it *shouldn't* be like that'. And then we may wonder why everything looks like the 'same old, dull old thing'. It will be because our awareness has become dull and stale.

We can 'get by' in our day-to-day lives with very little conscious awareness, if we allow ourselves to slip into this sleepy style of existence. Instead, we can shuffle along and day-dream – without even being aware of our dreams! We can become like automatons; automatically acting and responding in the same old way without examining and reflecting on anything that is happening in our lives.

We can travel to and from work without noticing much; we can do our daily chores, we can go round and round the same tracks with friends, spouse, family and colleagues as though we were playing a pre-recorded tape. We 'know' what we will say and do; we 'know' how other people will respond, and so (we believe) there is no need to pay much attention. We can operate our lives within rigid, relatively inflexible rules, with fixed roles and predictable outcomes. If we imprison ourselves in this way, there will be few surprises, and we will assume that we will be able to catch and deal with these. Eventually we can become so sluggish that only the most crude, exotic, dramatic, flamboyant, violent, extra-ordinary and extreme stimulus will gain our attention. (Hence the dreadful state of so much television and the popular press.) Anything that requires the mildest degree of subtlety of attention, or sustained attention and reflection will be lost to us.

In order to wake up a little, we don't have to go anywhere or do anything in particular; we don't have to become somebody else. We merely need to allow ourselves to notice that which we have already (unconsciously!) selected for attention. It is important to realise that we don't consciously decide what we are going to become conscious of! Indeed (think about it) we *can't* consciously decide, 'I'm going to be aware of this now'; because in the very process of saying this to ourselves we would have already become conscious of it!

Here, then, is a fascinating paradox. We don't, and can't in principle, consciously decide what we're going to become conscious of. The very act of 'becoming conscious' is something we have to trust and 'allow' to take care of itself unconsciously!

And so, in a way, this whole section about awareness is not so much addressed to the conscious mind – with lots of explicit strategems that we can consciously employ. It is more like a 'dig in the ribs', a jolt that will remind you to wake up on those occasions where it would be more appropriate for you to do so. You will need to trust that *you* will know – unconsciously – when it would be wise to become more conscious!

The power of the unconscious over the conscious can infuriate and surprise those who set so much store in being conscious about everything they do. The very root, substratum or foundation of our consciousness, it seems, is inaccessible to us; and here we are (some of us) hoping that we might be able to 'shine a torch' on everything. Thoughts come, without our thinking 'Next I'm going to think *that* thought'! – and how else could it be? Actions take place, without our necessarily having to think 'Now I'm going to do this'. And, even when we do think out our actions in advance of doing them, the connection (if any) between this thought/plan and the subsequent action is ultimately baffling to us! So it is that those everyday routine thoughts, and actions that seem so simple, under control and obvious to us are, when we investigate them, deeply mysterious. They become most under our control when we see that, in some difficult-to-pin-down sense, both the thoughts and the actions are not under our conscious control at all!

But perhaps we should leave it there, or else people might become thoroughly giddy about the simplest and most obvious train of thought and activity here before their very eyes! You may complain that life is dull and grey; and yet look again and you will see that the manner of operation of the most common-or-garden thought, feeling or action is deeply mysterious and fantastic beyond our wildest fantasy.

Action and awareness are amazing enigmas that quite defeat our conscious attempts to pin them all down and lay them all out before us. We may sometimes think about our actions, and think before we act. And this may (or may not) improve our control of what we do. It may help to make plans before we act; but these plans cannot, by their nature, be 'complete', or they would *be* the action.

I have a 'plan' of this book. But a complete plan of the book would be the book itself. Furthermore, I did not plan the plan! That came from nowhere. I was unconscious of it before it came. And so, too, will I stay unconscious of what I write next until I've written it. It doesn't necessarily help for me to run the sentences out in my head before I write them. It can be quicker, and more immediate and effective, to run them straight onto the paper. And so, in an *important* sense, I don't write this. I merely read and assess what gets written as the pen moves across the paper (or the fingers move across the keyboard). It is the same with all our seemingly obvious, 'well-controlled' and humdrum thoughts, feelings and actions. They are ultimately mysterious and enigmatic in the extreme.

We can, then, become obsessed about being aware of

everything in advance; and try too hard to make plans and be consciously aware of what we do. Many of our best ideas and inspiration can come 'from the blue'; 'just like that'; and we can sit like passive receivers of these mysterious, unpredictable, yet valuable, insights.

However, let's not make a fetish out of spontaneity and intuition. After all, many of our spontaneous and intuitive insights will turn out to be fallacious and foolish; useless and irrelevant delusions or fantasies.

Which kind of error are you most prone to make? Do you run into problems because you want everything consciously laid out and explained in your mind? Or do you get into difficulties because you think that your every 'intuition' is a priceless gem, a brilliant insight and a 'natural', precious, penetrating discovery?

Do you try too hard to explain, check, verify and prove everything? Or do you believe that whatever you 'intuit' is the Absolute Truth, that does not require any checking or verification?

Either road can lead to dogma and error. One kind of dogmatist thinks he knows because he's 'proved' everything and set it all out explicitly. The other thinks he knows because his 'natural intuition' has told him that his natural intuition is infallible!

63. I am **too aware**, too conscious and too self-conscious of everything I do.

Implicit in any study of psychology is the assumption that there is value in self-knowledge; and throughout these pages we have been exploring how much self-awareness may be of use to us. Consciousness of oneself is perhaps the crucial quality that differentiates us from other animals; and often we will not be able to choose alternative behaviour until we first become aware of just what it is that we are presently doing.

But it is worth remembering that most of what we do is done, and needs to be done, automatically and unconsciously, with very little awareness and attention on our part. Moreover, we would be able to accomplish very little if we always needed to be acutely aware of every single step we were taking. Conscious examination, assessment and re-evaluation are very valuable *sometimes*; but, if we tried to be conscious of everything we were doing, the examining and checking would get in the way of the doing, and we would get very little done and become very clumsy in our actions.

We can go wrong if we don't keep enough of an eye on our behaviour; but we can also run into difficulties if we expend too much time taking stock, keeping track, being very aware of every step, re-assessing every decision, checking and re-checking every action, motivation and intention.

If we try to be 'spectators' of everything we do, we probably won't do very much (and we won't get much pleasure from what we do achieve); and if we try to 'take a microscope' to our every single motive, intention and action we will probably find that we are left with inert and broken pieces of our conscious experience, with very little that lives, flows, moves or works.

Do *you* make the mistake of assuming that 'self-control' requires you to put a bright spot-light on every nook and cranny of motive and action? This notion is quite false, and it can lead to obsessive and self-obsessed behaviour where the person, in his desperate attempts to get more and more in control, in fact gets himself into ever more of a 'cramp'. He consequently loses quite a lot of whatever control he may have had.

A simple illustration is the story of the centipede who fell over himself when asked to describe accurately and exactly how he managed to walk with his one hundred legs.

In order to be in control of what we are doing, we often need to trust that it will work without checking or examining it. We need to let go of the action rather than hold on to it. If we let go, it will often fly well enough – seemingly of its own accord! But if we keep on holding our actions to us, in a desperate effort to check, examine and re-check everything, we will paralyse ourselves as we interfere with the action. We may even get ourselves into a potentially infinite regress, where we check the checking process, and then check that. There is theoretically no end to this process; but in fact it ends when, by checking, and checking and checking again, we grind ourselves to a complete standstill!

It is quite impossible, and undesirable, to be conscious of everything within and around us; and if you try too hard to be super-aware and super-controlled you will paralyse yourself.

Such paralysis is most apparent when we engage in physical activities that require skill, flexibility and a willingness to take risks. For example, a person who wants to be 'super-conscious' of every single little movement, and have a clear picture before, during and after every segment of action – is not likely to be much good at sporting activities of whatever sort. Some conscious examination and awareness of what you are doing is necessary of course; but at some stage you have got to let go and run, and jump, and just trust that your legs, feet and arms etc. will know what is needed of them.

In other words, you have to trust that you know what to do; but you have to remember that this (ever-mysterious) 'you' is also located in your body and not just in your conscious mind with its (occasionally) useful mental representations and re-constructions of experience.

The excessively mental person, who thinks that who he is is entirely located in his conscious mind, tends to hold his breath and hold his body in a defensive, somewhat cramped, posture; with a good deal of superfluous muscle-tension. This, he hopes, will help him to stay in control and prevent him from being taken by surprise. But in fact it merely keeps him stiff, clumsy, tense, anxious, paralysed, inflexible, exhausted and ineffective. Furthermore, this behaviour pattern can settle into a vicious cycle: The body becomes a place of chronic anxiety, chronic tension, chronic exhaustion and consequent clumsiness.

The over-controlling individual, sensing that he is in fact *losing* control, but failing to see why, tries harder and harder to achieve conscious mental control of his body. In fact all he is likely to be doing is withdrawing more of his attention into mental reflection and planning, rather than into immediate awareness of the dire warning messages that his body is likely to be sending him about this self-defeating physical abuse.

What all this amounts to is the fact that you can, in effect, try too much and too hard if you think that trying requires unremitting preparation, checking, conscious attention, internal dialogue, and a kind of neurotic holding on to yourself. When you say to someone "try harder, harder, HARDER!" you will often find that they clench their fists and jaw more and more, and tense up shoulders, stomach, arms and legs ever more tightly. This kind of 'trying' involves a lack of trust, a failure to realise that much that happens around and within us happens seemingly on its own, all by itself and *not* under our conscious control.

It is a very 'trying' experience to try to control everything in a premeditated, planned and conscious way, because it wastes a terrific amount of energy and it is essentially an ignorant and ineffective way of achieving control.

This is so even in relation to our conscious thoughts. If you try harder and harder to think, you will find that your thoughts in fact become more and more constricted and dull. We try and try to think the 'right' thoughts in the 'right' way, but how do you even know what you are going to think until you have thought it and, when you have done so, do you really need to think it again in order to be consciously in control? Do you have to, and can you, think what you are going to think?

The truth seems to be that thoughts come to us without our consciously bidding them. And so, although we can idly let our thoughts wander all over the place in a rather uncontrolled and undisciplined way (by failing to bring ourselves back to the task we have set ourselves), we can also lose control by trying to be too much in control. Ideas come to us and we can let them flow; and, if we are to be at all creative in what we do, we often need to let this flow of ideas happen without anticipating prematurely where it might lead to, and without constricting its development along narrow and pre-determined channels.

We can lose control if we don't try hard enough, *and* we can lose control if we try too hard. We fail to understand if we don't look consciously at what we are doing. *And* we can fail to understand if we attempt to be conscious of everything that we do.

Somewhere between these two positions we can find a middle way; and we'll be most effective if we don't try too hard to find it! Moreover, we may be most effective of all if we let this insight 'come to us'!

We cannot deal with any problem very well if we are spending too much time examining how well we are dealing with the problem. And so, for example, endlessly reading and re-reading a book on 'Problem-Solving Skills' (however useful that book may be) can never be a substitute for actually getting down to dealing with the problems themselves!

If we keep on trying to monitor our activity we interfere with the activity itself. For example, by saying to myself, "I'm really enjoying this", there's a danger that I shall take myself away from the pleasure; especially if I start to say "I want to keep this".

We will not 'find ourselves' by forever searching in the mirror or endlessly looking inside ourselves in deep introspection. 'We' are not some mysterious 'something' that we discover after uncovering layer after layer in a long inner journey of psychic exploration. No doubt there is a place for introspection, but the real self is not like some murky animal hiding under layers of rock and sand. Much of who we are is to be found not by constantly observing ourselves doing, or by sitting around in an armchair looking ever more deeply inwards. Rather, we 'find' much of ourselves through self-expression, by commitment, involvement, action, and co-operation with others. And this expression and activity only *sometimes* needs to be monitored, evaluated and assessed. Much of our time needs to be given over, not to talk and assessment, but to *action*!

64. I am having difficulty with the problem because, basically, I **don't want** to tackle it at all!

Do you believe that you should be absolutely of one mind about a problem and of your need to tackle it? Let's hope not, because it is very rare for us to be 'of one mind' about anything. On such unusual occasions we just go ahead and tackle our problems and, no matter how complex, risky, or difficult they may be, we go forward without delay, regret, doubt, distraction or deviation.

Much more often, though, you will have complaints, regrets, doubts and all the rest; and these will, to some extent, seem to get in the way of your tackling the problem and make it more difficult for you to deal with it. You will then probably call the problem itself a 'difficult' one; but the difficulty will in fact lie within your own conflictual response to it rather than to anything inherent in the problem itself.

It is wise to have respect and regard for all our reactions, and to try to learn from them. We will then, if this seems necessary, respectfully, patiently and calmly over-rule our objections and complaints and go ahead and tackle the problem with all the determination we can muster. We will over-rule our internal opposition; but we should not seek to, and cannot, over-whelm it!

However, it does sometimes happen that, after we have made a definite decision to do something, we later decide that we have made the wrong decision. Our complaints and objections continue and strengthen. We become ever more sluggish and reluctant to tackle the problem. No matter how much we feel guilty about our laggardly approach, our objections and criticisms grow. We may even feel guilty because we *are* tackling it! (Yes, it does happen; a person can feel guilty when they *do* do something, and then, when they stop, they feel guilty because they've stopped!)

Obviously, there are times when we need to reassess our original decision; and we may decide that we've made a mistake and that we shouldn't have tackled the problem in the first place.

The most difficult decisions are those where the arguments and counter-arguments are stacked up almost exactly equally. Sometimes it can seem as though it is arbitrary which way we should move. And sometimes, indeed, it is pretty well a case of 'six and two threes'. In such circumstances we may indeed do best by spinning a coin to determine our decision! We will then at least be able to start taking some action, and if we find that the coin comes up with what we then feel strongly to have been the wrong answer, we will at least have been able to use the coin to find out what we really *did* want to do!

It is, needless to say, important to be sensitive to the 'pros' and 'cons' involved in decision-making, but, when the balance of argument is only very slight, and can seem to tilt from one option to another almost from day to day, then we can actually become *too* sensitive to the subtle nuances of the argument.

It is useful to compare this human process of dithering and

endlessly changing one's mind to the way in which a thermostat functions. A thermostat, just to remind you, switches an electrical supply on or off depending on a (pre-set) temperature range. Above a certain temperature it switches off. Below a (lower) temperature, it switches the electrical circuit on again. This is all very well, but if the 'switch on' temperature is too close to the 'switch off' level, ie. the system is too sensitive to only very slight temperature changes, then the whole system can be thrown into chaos, and lose its overall effectiveness. It will be constantly switched on and off, and thus switched off again before the 'switch-on' cycle has been fully completed.

This sort of thing happens with 'super-sensitive' individuals faced with more than one task that needs to be tackled at any one time. As soon as they begin one job they start to think that they should switch over to another that (perhaps equally) demands their attention. They thus switch over and change their minds before they've made any real progress with the first problem. Thus, via a self-defeating sequence of hops from one problem to the next, they end up with a superficial examination of everything but get nothing much done at all, despite their ever more desperate efforts to make progress!

65. I am **undisciplined** in the way that I tackle this problem.

Discipline is a most important, and most abused and mis-understood concept. It tends to be associated with a harsh, repressive, unforgiving, inflexible, guilt-ridden and domineering style of behaviour. But such self-hating puritanism does not in fact do much to improve our ability to control either ourselves or anyone else. On the contrary, it confuses, fragments, damages and immobilises us so that we end up being even less in control and less aware of the real nature of discipline.

Really, the whole of this book is an exploration of what it might be to take a more disciplined approach to problem-solving; because discipline is, if you like, an 'umbrella' concept that involves most of the more detailed topics I have explored elsewhere.

Sadly, we so often seem to be stuck with either the Puritanical or the Libertarian conception of discipline. The Puritan says "What we need is more *discipline*: the country's falling apart at the seams...; In my day..." etc. etc. and unwittingly uses talk of discipline as a means of expressing or releasing his own anger, frustration and fears about all that he sees as wrong with society. Discipline, for the Puritan, is the harsh regime; the uncompromising stand, the fierce, hostile, unrelenting attack on all that is 'bad' and 'wrong'.

The Puritanical conception of self-discipline requires that we flagellate ourselves and feel an underlying shame at much of what we do. We persecute and repress ourselves, rather than learn from all our 'bad' and 'wrong' fantasies, impulses and intentions. Because of this, those repressed parts conduct an eternal, destructive, exhausting guerilla war against those bastion/fortress parts of ourselves that we deem to be good and right. (Thus, see also section twenty-five on Guilt.)

Such behaviour is not really discipline. Rather, it is revenge, righteous wrath, unacknowledged fear, uncertainty and insecurity; a scarcely veiled anger and hostility. None of it helps to promote a proper understanding of discipline, or a genuine ability to exert self-control. It is indeed an essentially *un*-disciplined and ineffective indulgence of (generally unconsious) feelings and impulses!

The other common, and equally inaccurate perception of discipline is the libertarian or hedonistic view. The libertarian has the same conception of discipline as the Puritan. However, his attitude towards it is different, since he recognises that this Puritan conception is essentially destructive, repressive, life-denying and constricting.

The libertarian consequently reacts against discipline, seeing it as repressive and authoritarian. Thus the libertarian cry: "Away with all this repressive discipline; let there be Freedom; let us each express and create for ourselves; let us each realise our own potential and not allow ourselves to be constricted and trammelled by any life-killing discipline".

"I do my thing, you do yours. And if we meet that's beautiful. And if we don't, it can't be helped."*

The trouble with this kind of anarchism is that it does not help people to find or express themselves; it does not help us to find ways of co-existing with others; and it does not help to create a society that supports and nurtures its citizens. On the contrary, far from helping us to be free, it allows people to become slaves of their own whims, fancies, selfish impulses, amoral individualistic fantasies and childish behaviour.

With such a libertarian avoidance of discipline, we do not find ourselves; rather we find that an undisciplined selfish hedonism leads to pain, chaos, endless avoidable and unnecessary error, and longer term suffering as a result of short term folly. We end up with a 'human potential' whose development has stayed stuck at the level of infantile egocentricity.

Such an anarchic conception of freedom does not free us and does not lead us to become 'beautiful people'. On the contrary, we become selfish and self-centred monsters, readily intoxicated and distracted by shallow pleasures, easy indulgences and quick cure-all remedies and answers. With this kind of freedom, all that we can ever express is, at best, a reflection of the shallowness and immaturity that such freedom creates. Self-expression requires not simply the absence of (certain) constraints, it also demands genuine self-discipline and 'training' of many sorts. For example, if we are to express ourselves, by whatever means of expression, we need to learn *how* to make effective use of whatever medium we have chosen. Thus it is that all the various branches of the Arts, Sciences and Humanities are (quite correctly) described as ... disciplines.

The anarchic individualist is conscious of the ways in which authoritarianism can crush human individuality but, because (s)he puts the individual on the altar at the expense of society as a whole, he fails to see how a society, at its best, is a means of supporting and protecting individual and collective rights. The trouble is that 'human potential' anarchism lays so much stress on individual *rights* that it fails to see that there can be no rights, and no society, without individual duties, and social and moral *obligations*.

*(Fritz Perls, one of the gurus of the Human Potential Movement of the 1960s.)

Needless to say, the problem of balancing individual and collective rights and obligations has, and always will be, a painfully difficult task for all of us, and one that we are unlikely to 'solve' finally and absolutely. The libertarian, however, does not even try to grapple with the problem, and does not even seem to realise that this process of balancing between individual and group demands is a challenge that we must all face. Consequently, in his anthems to selfishness and self-obsession, he unwittingly creates a society that is amoral and, for all his talk of 'sensitivity' and 'caring', his behaviour is essentially uncaring and irresponsible with damaging social consequences.

If we simply allow ourselves to focus on 'personal power' and 'personal expression' then, whether we realise it or not, we will create a society where power ultimately congregates in the hands of the most powerful and ruthless and where, in the process of this taking place, life becomes 'nasty, brutish and short'.

There are many social patterns and movements to be observed in the study of history, and one that quite commonly seems to occur is this oscillation back and forth between Repressive Authoritarianism and Indulgent Libertarianism. Each feeds off and reacts against the excesses of its opposite, but each is essentially undisciplined and destructive. Will we ever learn? The answer, probably, is 'yes'; we've learned this lesson many times and then, just as often, we forget!

With a (genuinely) disciplined approach, we can learn to:

Face up to difficult problems rather than run away from them. (Section one)

Tolerate *confusion*. (Section two)

Take *risks* and allow for *mistakes*. (Section four)

Avoid *distraction* (Sections three and eight) and *delay*. (Section ten)

Be *energetic* (Sections thirteen and sixteen) yet *tentative*. (Section seven)

Be *self-reliant*. (Section sixty-seven)

Ensure that *long-term well-being* triumphs over short-term comfort and gratification. (Section eleven)

Go after the *root* cause of problems. (Anatomy of Errors)

Be *persistent*, (Section thirteen), *decisive* (Section fifteen) and *hopeful*. (Section seventeen)

Avoid *going it alone*. (Section sixty-seven)

Be *trusting*. (Section forty-five)

Achieve both *confidence*. (Section nineteen) and *competence*. (Section twenty-eight)

Avoid being too *dependent on the approval of others*. (Section twenty)

Be *tolerant* (Section fifty-eight), *forgiving*, (Section forty-six and forty-seven), *compassionate*, (Section forty-nine), *understanding*, (whole book), *respectful*. (Section fifty-one)

Be both *proud* and *ashamed* as appropriate. (Section twenty-five)

Be *clear* and *systematic* (whole book); taking a *step by step* approach with both long-term and short-term goals. (Section eleven)

Distinguish between *urgent* and *important* problems. (Section twenty-nine)

Go *one step* at a time. (Section thirty)

Avoid perfectionism; be *realistic* (Section thirty-one); make *compromises*. (Section thirty-eight)

Avoid simplistic 'answers'. (Section thirty-two)

Be flexible (Section thirty-eight); accept limitations. (Section thirty-one)

Understand and enjoy *good humour*. (Section thirty-five)

Avoid *repression* (Section thirty-six) and *indulgence*. (Section thirty-seven)

Be open-minded. (Section thirty-three)

Seek to achieve a non-repressive, compassionate control of anger, irritation, resentment, excessive pride, arrogance, selfishness and *self-centredness*. (Section sixty-five)

Be *out-going* (Section forty-four), avoid *blame* (Section forty-six), bitterness, (Section forty-seven), greed, (Section forty-eight). Control domineering, spiteful, revengeful and *malicious behaviour*. (Section forty-nine)

Cultivate *patience*. (Section fifty)

Be assertive. (Section fifty-one)

Utilise and welcome *'good' luck* and accept, learn from, and come to terms with, *'bad' luck* – without seeking 'supernatural' explanations. (Section fifty-three)

Seek to understand and cultivate *honesty-with-tact*. (Section fifty-four)

Take a more *relaxed* approach. (Section fifty-five)

Tolerate and act skillfully with *conflict*. (Section fifty-six)

Tolerate *set-backs*. (Section fifty-eight)

Realise that 'work' is not an inevitable obstacle to self-expression, but is a potential and necessary *means* of self-expression. (Section sixty-eight)

This is not a complete list; but it is long enough! The last few sections in this book will, among other things, seek to deepen and round off our understanding of this, most crucial, topic – *Discipline*.

Let us, though, for once and for all demolish the idea that to be disciplined is to be joyless, humourless, unforgiving and inflexible. On the contrary, there is little joy for those who will not constrain themselves at all, nor much happiness for those who constrict themselves too much. Yet again a difficult balance needs to be found, but there is potentially an enormous reward for us if we can find it – for ourselves *and* others.

66. I had a **troubled childhood**, and my recent past has been difficult; this lies at the root of my problem.

How far can you realistically expect to be able to make any substantial changes in your experience and behaviour? Are you now irrevocably set in your ways? Is your behaviour immutably fixed by your heredity – your genetic inheritance? Was it 'set in plaster' as a result of that happened to you in (say) the first ten or twenty years of your life?

Clearly, this entire book rests on the assumption that change *is* possible, since there would be little point in looking at underlying motives, and explaining alternative options, if there was no possibility of our being able to do anything about them. Hence my working assumption that we *can* change – far more than we think – but far *less* than we'd like!

Obviously, though, our past history and genetic make-up have an enormous influence over what we do and don't do. Any changes that take place must do so within these constraints rather than despite them.

The difficulty is that we simply do not know the extent of these genetic and environmental influences. For example, people have, for years, asked "Which is most important; 'Nature' (heredity) or 'Nurture' (upbringing)?" . . . In the hope that we could in principle come up with some answer that specified proportionate influences; (eg. '50 : 50' or '80 : 20' or whatever). The trouble is that this question is probably unanswerable in principle (and maybe the question is misplaced) because 'nature' and 'nurture' do not exist as separate influences, but interact.

We all begin our lives with a genetic inheritance, but we do not know how influential (for good or ill) our environment *could* be. It really depends on the limits of our creative potential; and since 'potential' is, by definition, not 'actual' it is somewhat difficult to measure it!

Certainly, the range of achievement and non-achievement to be observed so far in the history of humanity is very large! There is no reason at all to think that we have reached our limits, and so there is no way of knowing how far we can build upon or overcome environmental and genetic influences.

We all of us go around with self-defeating attitudes, destructive and unhelpful habits, and clumsy, ineffective and painful styles of behaviour. We all, to a greater or lesser extent, are deficient in skills and disciplines that would serve us well if we could (or would) but master them. And clearly all of this is influenced by the kind of upbringing we had; the way we were treated by key people in our early lives – parents, teachers, other family, friends and so on. Parental influences generally seem to be the most important (hardly surprising); and the key foundation stones of behaviour, thought and feeling seem to get laid within the first seven years or so.

Nonetheless, there are some people who, by exploring these major past influences, and actively working towards alternatives, have made enormous changes in their lives and have moved on from what might have appeared to have been insuperable handicaps, barriers and constraints.

The pessimist might say that only a small minority could ever manage to make significant changes, whereas the optimist will suggest that such a minority could, and should, be taken as an inspiring and empowering example for others to follow. We cannot infer what *might be* possible from what has been actual so far.

This book has explored a large variety of ways in which we can make a problem out of problems, as a result of the ways in which we tackle them. It has looked at the process of problem-solving rather than the content of any particular problem and, I hope, this kind of unravelling of the ways in which we can, and do, tackle problems will help you, the reader, to put at least some of the principles spelt out here into practice in your own life.

In the process of doing this, you may be triggered into remembering just how and where some of your more ineffective problem-solving strategies were first learned. Some psychologists and psychotherapists insist that it is crucial that you first unravel past influences if you are to be able to move on from them, while others assert that the most important thing to do is to get a clear picture of alternative (more effective) ways of behaving, with a realistic strategy of step-by-step change. Each side in this controversy tends to stridently insist that they have the answer, but there is not yet any clear or conclusive evidence to settle the matter one way of the other.

A self-help book like this will tend to focus on present behaviour and alternative options, because useful generalisation can be made about these. It is much more difficult to generalise about where these behaviours originate. Each of us has his own more or less unique mix of past influences and experiences.

In other words, I can spell out here some of the ways in which you can make an unnecessary problem out of problems, and I can indicate (within the severe limits of space) what alternatives are available. What I cannot do is tell you just how it was that you personally came to take on these self-defeating attitudes to problems. But, in any case, I am uncertain about how far this really matters. There are some who insist that it is crucially important for us to each look at our own past, and the influences that this has had, and is having, on us. Others, though, say that what really matters is that we look to the *future*, and work practically and realistically towards achieving the goals we have set ourselves. Probably we need to do both.

67. I am having difficulties with this problem because I am trying too much to **go it alone**.

The danger of writing a book on self-help of one sort or another is that people can wrongly infer that they ought to be doing everything by themselves. Generally we tend to read books on our own, but most of what is within these pages might best be achieved if it were tackled with others; in discussion, in groups; with the give and take, exchange of ideas and feeling, personal contact, mutual support and inspiration that we can give and get from other people.

No doubt we can rely too much on others and fail to stand on our own feet. But it is also true that we can cut ourselves off too much from others, so that we neither give nor receive sufficiently from them. Instead, we can pretend that to be responsible means that we must always 'go it alone'.

We each have the last word on our own decisions, whether we realise it or not. But these decisions are not made in a social vacuum, and they have social consequences. Moreover, if they are to be made wisely, we would do well to consult the opinions of others whose views we respect. No one can be an 'authority' for me unless I choose to recognise that they have something of value to offer me. But it would be perverse and foolish of me to ignore what others can give, and to pretend that I am totally self-sufficient.

A good deal of support that we can give to, and receive from, others lies not so much in practical advice (there tends to be a glut of this). More desirable, is a willingness to give attention, show concern, support and an underlying respect for other people and their problems. This can renew and inspire without encroaching upon them. Often, all we need from others is a recognition and regard for ourselves and the problems we face. We don't want other people to solve our problems for us, but we do want respect, understanding and support, so that we ourselves can find the strength to cope. We want others to help us to 'do it for ourselves'.

This book, I hope, provides just one, limited, form of support. It doesn't offer neat answers (there aren't any!) and it leaves huge gaps because it examines a large number of questions in a limited space. Moreover, it is, at the end of the day, *your* job to fill in the gaps and decide on the actions.

No matter how useful any book may be, I want to stress that *no* book can be a substitute for the kind of direct, face to face, support that we can get (and *need* to get) from friends and others.

68. I approach my problems in the **wrong spirit**.

What is it to approach problems in the 'right spirit'; and does this 'spirit' have anything to do with the spiritual dimension that some consider to have been lacking in recent years?

Any talk of 'spirituality' causes many people to back off in the expectation that this is going to be about phantoms, fantasies, supernatural experience, dogma, the occult, deities and medieval claims to Absolute Knowledge and Final Answers. Speaking personally, I must say that I am not much impressed with 'the spiritual' if this is taken to be a set of rather dubious, and untested, claims to certain knowledge, magical powers, exotica, ecstatic experiences and the like.

We can feel ecstatic at times and, goodness knows, there is nothing wrong with that! But to organise our lives so that they become a search for 'peak experiences', or final answers, or magic powers or ghouls and ghosts, benevolent or otherwise, seems to me to involve a failure to face up to life as it really is, with its change, uncertainty and limitation.

To search for 'the miraculous' and the magical presupposes that this ordinary life is not already miracle and magic enough; and to look for 'final answers' assumes that we can finally tie everything up and keep it all fixed and unchanging.

The chase after peak experiences has become big business in recent years; but too often it is assumed that there is something wrong with feeling low, or stuck, or depressed. Furthermore, in the very process of frenetically searching for joy, we take ourselves still further away from savouring the joys that do exist, but which are often to be found within and intermingled with our misery rather than *despite* it.

I am not much interested in 'spirits' as ghostly phantoms; be they hiding in the flowers, the attic, or anywhere else. And I tend to put them into the same category as fairies, Snow White and Father Christmas. But I am very interested in the underlying *spirit* with which we tackle ourselves and our lives. By this I don't mean anything supernatural, but merely the most fundamental principles and foundations upon which we organise, and make sense of, ourselves, our experience, beliefs, feelings and behaviour.

In what spirit do *you* live your life ...?

* As a preparation for some 'better' life to come?
* As a mystery to be explored?
* An adventure?
* A tragedy?
* Comedy of errors?
* Epic?
* Farce?
* Soap Opera?
* A meaningless ritual?
* A sick joke?
* A prison?
* Meaningless torture?
* A steady progression 'onwards and upwards'?
* ... all of these?

In what spirit do you look upon yourself ...?

* As separate from and at odds with others?
* As in a 'rat race' against others?
* As part of a 'brotherhood and sisterhood' of humanity?
* As part of a greater unity in a living, mysterious universe?

* As vulnerable and insecure?
* As armed and armoured against others?
* As conquerer of an inanimate World?
* As supported and nurtured by the World?
* As a part of what the World is doing?
* As a process rather than an entity?
* As essentially wicked and evil?
* As an insignificant speck of no value?
* As the most important person in the world?
* As potentially good and caring, loving and loveable?

Why do you do what you do...?

* To grab as much as you can for yourself regardless of others?
* To express yourself, to unfold your own potential and inspire the potential in others?
* To protect yourself; to cover yourself against attacks from others?

How do you communicate?

* You are essentially honest-and-tactful?
* You often lie, rationalise and cheat?

How do you see others?

* As hostile competitors that you must use, exploit, out-manoeuvre, manipulate, dominate and undermine?
* As human beings like yourself who you can love, respect and support; and who can love, respect and support you?

How do you see the future?

* As more or less hopeless?
* As a grey continuation of the past?
* As a meaningless repetition of previous errors?
* As an effortless progression?
* As a difficult but challenging source of hope, faith, opportunity and adventure?

What do you think of what you know about yourself and your world?

* It is utterly and absolutely certain?
* It is something you must cling to for your very survival?
* It is utterly useless?
* It is useful, but partial, limited, temporary and subject to change?

How do you deal with conflict?

* As catastrophic and dreadful?
* As a battle that you must win at all costs?
* As a challenge and opportunity to give and take?
* As a means to learn and teach and preserve goodwill, mutual respect and integrity?

What are you seeking? What are you trying to do with your life?

* Just trying to survive?
* Fame and fortune?
* Service to others?
* Self expression?
* Self transcendence?
* Success? Power? Love? Attention? Celebrity? Certainty? A long rest? A safe and predictable routine? Ecstacy? Drama? A challenge? A fight to the death?

What feelings often lie beneath the surface inside you?

* Rage? Hatred? Terror? Boredom? Hilarity? Hope? Despair? Exuberance? Awe? Wonder? Scepticism? Insecurity? Tolerance? Patience? Trust? Confidence? Reliance? Dependence?...?

What short phrase(s) would best describe you?

* Being the Best and Beating the Rest?
* Almost Made It?

* Battered but never broken?
* Poor Me?
* Lost then Found?
* Happy ever after?
* Pride before the Fall?
* Martyr?
* Unsung Hero/Heroine?
* Wolf in sheep's clothing?
* Damaged beyond repair?
* A Nonentity?
* A Miracle of Life?

How do you look upon Love?

* A source of safety and security?
* An illusion?
* A romantic indulgence?
* An exhausting irrelevance?
* A mysterious key to life?
* In opposition to Power?
* In need of, and needed for, Power?
* A source of endless surprise?
* An inspiration?
* A way of getting what I want?
* Something I can barter?
* Something I must keep for my friends alone?
* An impossible ideal?
* A means of escape?
* A way of passing the time?
* Another word for Sex?
* An ethereal, other worldly abstraction?
* A four letter word?

Western Culture seeems to have rather lost track of its spiritual roots; not so much in the sense that we no longer hold on to certain theological beliefs about life, the universe etc., but more importantly in the sense that we don't bother sufficiently to trouble ourselves to examine and care about the underlying spirit with which we live our lives – in terms of the kinds of questions sketched out above.

There *is* an underlying spirit that tends to predominate; and it is all the more powerful because we don't pay attention to it and we fail to ask ourselves how far it is doing us any good. This seems so often to be the spirit of material acquisitiveness, greed, selfishness, competitiveness, defensiveness, aggression, exploitation, underlying insecurity, hostility and associated attitudes, feelings and behaviour. We would do well to ask ourselves, more often, just where such deep-seated principles come from, how they are nurtured and what we could do to change them.

It shouldn't, by now, take much to recognise that a spirit of goodwill, toleration, love, compassion, open-mindedness, flexibility, trust, co-operation and respect is far more likely to serve us well than the previous sad list. Yet, though we recognise all of this, putting it into practice in our daily lives is, always was, and perhaps always will be, quite another matter; and we have explored many of the reasons for this in the last few hundred pages.

The underlying spirit with which we approach problems is at least as important as any detailed account of technique or strategy. For it is the basic 'bed-rock' upon which everything else rests.

With the right spirit we can find our 'heaven on earth'; but not in the sense of having all our ideals turned into reality. (This is most unlikely to happen and, if it ever did, we would probably find that after all we didn't like the result!) However, with the 'right spirit', we would be more able to 'breathe out', let ourselves go within, jump into, allow, accept and be fundamentally at peace with – the world as it actually is. (Which is, after all, the only world that is available to us!) This would not mean that we became tired and flaccid fatalists. On the contrary. After all, part of what the world is, is *ourselves*, with all our dreams, schemes, fears, pain, insecurity, intentions, energies and efforts.

With such a spirit of faith in ourselves, our world and others, we could move and act with grace; we could become enlightened enough to abandon the search for final 'enlightenment'; we could be alive enough to let each previous moment die so as to allow each 'new dawn'; we could feel at one with others in our separateness, and cease to make an effort out of *effort*, or see an obstacle in *obstacles* or a disharmony in *conflict*. We could let the 'ordinary' be miracle enough, and have faith enough to live without 'final answers' or 'final certainties'. We could have enough equilibrium and balance within ourselves to give up expecting that we should always feel balanced and in equilibrium!

All this is, of course, easy (enough) to describe, but much more difficult to achieve. Moreover, it is unrealistic and self-defeating to think that we ever can, must, or will finally 'do it'. There is no Final Salvation or Final Resting Place (for as long as we are still alive!), but we can at least see if we can make a slightly better job of tackling the next 'problem' and savour each moment regardless of how well it fits in with our plans.

69. I am having difficulties with this problem because tackling it seems a **pointless, meaningless** exercise.

Philosophers and theologians have, from time immemorial asked "what is the meaning and purpose of our lives?" and all manner of answers have been explored. It would be quite outside the range of this book to try to do justice to any of these investigations.

Conversely, the life of the overly reflective individual can feel equally meaningless because, if all you ever do is try to ask what does life *mean*, you will discover that such a limited activity itself becomes meaningless!

The action-oriented individual does not *think* about meaning and purpose; but *feels* a sense of purpose within *the very process* of taking action. The more introspective, reflective, individual, with an orientation towards theory, realises that action alone is not sufficient and knows that one needs, from time to time, to sort out one's actions and options in order to make them meaningful.

The trouble is, though, that the theoretician can be in danger of spending so much time trying to sort out what he is doing, that he gives himself no time to actually *do* anything. Thus he tries to theorise about what he does, or might do, but has little to theorise about and reflect upon given that he does so little. He becomes a voyeur of life rather than a full participant; and it is a soul-destroying (and meaning-destroying) experience if you only ever *observe* yourself and other people without ever actively *expressing* yourself or engaging with others!

On the other hand, we do now need to pay some heed to this question of meaning and purpose since, like anything else, tackling problems of any sort can only be done within some sort of framework by means of which we try to make sense of our existence.

Some people plunge into whatever seems to be available in the day-to-day challenges that face them, deriving some satisfaction from this, and scarcely ever taking a 'longer view' of what they are doing. Others are so keen to get an overall perspective on what they are doing that they spend too much time in abstract reflection and too little on concrete action. Their abstract ideas then become somewhat arid and vacuous since they have so little practical experience from which to develop ideas that have any real flesh and blood in them.

Life can eventually seem meaningless to us if we plunge endlessly into day-to-day actions without ever trying to take stock of what we are doing. The action-oriented individual may spend years tackling and chasing one task and attraction after the next without giving any of it much of a thought. But sooner or later (s)he is likely to feel the need to ask "What does all this *mean*? Where am I going with all of this?".

The theoretically inclined individual sometimes takes the view that the meaning and purpose of our actions always need to be sorted out before we can sensibly take any action. Thus he spends a great deal of time trying to figure out what he should do and why, and tries to get an impeccable picture of all this. The theoretician too often believes that meaning and purpose must be discovered by a process of reasoning, reflection and abstract study and that all this must be properly clarified before our actions can be sensible, meaningful and informed. Too much abstract speculation of this sort, though, eventually becomes arid and sterile.

As a consequence, the theoretical investigator sometimes decides that, ultimately, life is absurd and meaningless; that, at the bottom of everything, there lies a great hopeless, useless, vacuum. Such a pessimistic existentialist takes the view that 'smaller minded' people, who busy themselves in day-to-day pleasures and challenges, are missing the 'ultimate truth' of existence.

Some restless souls travel the globe in their minds or, increasingly these days, in actual fact. They search and search for people, places and activities that would give them a sense of meaning and purpose. They want to see a perfect blue-print of the way their life should be before they will set about building it.

Others stay exactly where they are born and make an immediate commitment to the people, environment and challenges that are closest to them. They build their lives without any blue-print; and the meaning of their life grows and is discovered within the action.

Many people are searching everywhere in order to discover what their life means; as though they might find the answer hidden away in some tree stump in a golden cask containing a secret scroll! Meaning is not discovered in this way; it is created by our willingness to commit ourselves to action and to what the action reveals. We can, and should, reflect on what it is to be human, but there can be no *being*-in-the-world without *doing*-in-the-world. With consciousness of our 'being' we can see where we are going and why; but only in the doing do we go anywhere.

Awareness helps us to see, but action is the locomotive of existence without which we feel no exhilaration and go nowhere. Thought and perception provide us with consciousness and insight, but action furnishes us with something for thought to be conscious of! Action without thought is shallow and ill-informed; thought without action is empty and sterile. And, most important, meaning only arises when both are acting together!

> The aggravated angst of the arid intellectual
> Blocked up with thoughts and his sighing gas fire
> Was blown with the leaves in the Autumn Season
> Yellow like them and ready to expire.
>
> Then he, like a child, with no need for a Reason
> Moved cool and calm, and was lifted from the mire.
>
> He had searched and searched for an academic lair
> But the 'answer', he found, lay in simple *fresh air!*

It is not for any of us to tell others what meaning they are to find in their lives (though plenty have always volunteered answers and many more have always asked for them!). We create meaning in our action and awareness of what we do, and each of us is responsible for our own creation. (Though, needless to say, such a creation of meaning – like the creation of anything else – is done in a world full of constraints!)

Some will say that if meaning is merely created then life really *is* meaningless! Such a pessimistic conclusion will only seem true, though, to those who have never tasted the experience of finding meaning and fulfilment in committed action and exploration. We come alive and find a sense of purpose when we have faith enough in ourselves and the world around us to send the locomotive of our soul forward into the ultimate mystery of tomorrow even though we know we have only a partial and fragmented map of what tomorrow might bring.

Many lack this faith, and instead substitute it for the various forms of dogmatic pseudo-faith which generally state that tomorrow will be pretty much like today only better (if you are good!). This is a childish, and erroneous, conception of faith and shows a lack of maturity.

Throughout history people have been searching for Final Answers that will give them a sense of meaning and purpose, and while many have purported to provide such answers, many others have indicated how futile this is. There was the Zen monk who was asked by a disciple: "Master, what must I do to achieve enlightenment?" The monk replied, "Have you finished your meal?" and when his disciple answered in the affirmative the monk gave his 'final answer' that reverberates down the centuries: "Then go and wash your bowl!"*

I do hope that the meaning and simple wisdom of this 'action-research' approach to existence will have come across to readers without their feeling the need to get obssessed with the washing up – thus making an idolatorous fetish of 'simple purity' in action. (I myself now use a dishwasher, which, of course, provides no more of a 'final answer' than anything else.)

The reflective and open-minded individual cannot help but notice that what we 'know' about anything vanishes into utter insignificance when compared with what we *don't* know. Our knowledge functions mainly as a way of showing us just how little we know, and will ever know. Some see this as just too painful to bear, and thus shelter behind dogma and idolatory of one sort or another. (We can be just as idolatorous with intellectual idols as people used to be with wooden varieties.) Others, though, live with fulfilment, meaning and purpose, and are open to all the joys and miseries, fullness and emptiness of life, without needing to pretend that they have found the last word on anything.

We don't need to have, or to wish for, a final answer. The zest we can feel at the prospect of a new day tomorrow is very much the result, not of what we *know* will happen. Rather, it arises from our knowledge that we don't know what the future will bring, and don't know what shape, meaning, purpose and sense of identity we will be able to wrest from it! Therein lies the raw terror and rich excitement of being alive!

*(Quoted in Alan Watts, *The Way of Zen*)

Conclusion

We have looked, albeit briefly, at sixty-nine ways in which we can make a problem out of problems; whereby we tackle them with less skill and grace than we are capable of, and consequently get ourselves into difficulties that we might otherwise have avoided. In so doing, we have looked at the *process* of problem-solving rather than the *content* of particular problems. Hopefully, you can apply much of this to specific problems that you presently face and will face in the future; so that you can be just a little more skilful, warm and wise in your approach.

I do not pretend that putting theory into practice is easy, or that there is any infallible method for doing this. Neither do I pretend to be an advanced student in all of this! On the contrary, a major reason for writing the book was because it has helped me to sort out and clarify a few issues for myself. It has helped me, and I hope it can be of use to you.

We have examined a considerable amount of information in a very short space. The virtue of this approach, I think, is that it allows us to sketch extremely important interconnections between what are seemingly diverse topics. The snag is that we are limited in how far we can amplify, follow through and give practical illustration and more detailed hints that might be of value. Further illustration would make the book far too long, and people would be wiser to follow through specific areas for themselves, with others, and through further reading of their own.

If some of what has been said seems like 'common sense' then I don't apologise for that. As far as I can see, common sense is rather rarely practised, and I think it is useful to remind ourselves, and each other, rather more often, about what we already know in our hearts.

Suggested Reading

Richard Bandler, *Using Your Brain – for a Change*, Real People's Press, (U.S.A), 1985

Richard Bandler and John Grinder, *Reframing*, Real People's Press, (U.S.A.), 1982

Aaron Beck, *Cognitive Therapy and Emotional Disorders*, New American Library, 1976

Windy Dryden (ed), *Individual Therapy in Britain*, Harper & Row, 1984

Wayne W. Dyer, *Your Erroneous Zones*, Sphere, 1979

Ram Dass & Paul Gorman, *How Can I Help?*, Rider, 1985

Sheila Ernst & Lucy Goodison, *In Our Own Hands: A Book of Self-Help Therapy*, Women's Press, 1981

Piero Ferrucci, *What We May Be*, Turnstone (Thorsons), 1982

Alex Howard, *Finding a Way: A Realistic Introduction to Self-Help Therapy*, Gateway, 1985

Richard Nelson-Jones, *The Theory and Practice of Counselling Psychology*, Holt, Rinehart & Winston, 1982

Janette Rainwater, *You're in Charge*, Turnstone (Thorsons), 1981

Virginia Satir, *Peoplemaking*, Souvenir Press, 1983

Gail Sheehy, *Passages: Predictable Crises of Adult Life*, Corgi, 1977

Some other GATEWAY BOOKS that might interest you.

Finding a Way: *A Realist's Introduction to Self-Help Therapy*
by Alex Howard

"This exceptionally helpful and down-to-earth book is a revealing, teach yourself course in removing those masks we hide behind, in getting to know ourselves and others better . . . providing many practical guidelines of who we really are and how much we can truly give to each other. I strongly recommend this valuable book". *Science of Thought Review.*

224pp   *paper*   £5.95 *(US $11.95)*

Towards a Magical Technology
by Tom Graves

Here is a challenge to the narrow vision of contemporary science. Tom Graves is not interested in theories, but as a technologist in making things work. Much true creativity has an intuitive origin and this book examines synchronicities and magic as they operate in the creative field. This controversial book draws from dowsing to computers, from radical psychology to subatomic physics.

96pp *illus.* *paper* £3.95 *(US $8.95)*

Fruits of the Moon Tree: *The Medicine Wheel and Transpersonal Psychology* by Alan Bleakley

The psychological process of maturation, by which each of us must come to terms with the masculine and feminine within us, is described in this major work. Drawing on images of Celtic lore, of classical mythology and fairy tale, archetypes and dreams, Alan Bleakley relates these to North American Indian Medicine Wheel teachings which stress the healing qualities of plants, animals, the earth — Nature herself.

320pp *120 illus.* *paper* £6.95 *(US $13.95)*

Living in Time: *Experiencing Time Cycles with Astrology*
by Palden Jenkins

This provides a language for the understanding of the nature of Time as it unfolds in our lives, suitable for beginners, samplers, reassessors and growing souls. Lunar cycles, planetary motions, time cycles and crunch points, birth charts and change are all examined with a new eye, written in a simple style, encouraging creativity and involvement. There are lots of illustrations, diagrams and projects.

224pp *120 illus.* *paper* £6.95 *(US $13.95)*

Something is Happening: *Spiritual Awareness and Depth Psychology in the New Age*   by Winifred Rushforth

A book of profound wisdom that has already achieved the status of a classic, it shows how the spiritual and psychological ways of understanding are one; both bound up with the healing process that must take place before we can become mature and whole human beings. Winifred Rushforth pioneered therapeutic and creative groupwork in Scotland where she was well known for her religious broadcasts.

160pp   *paper*   £4.95   *(US $9.95)*

Earth's Embrace: *Facing the Shadow of the New Age*
by Alan Bleakley

This is a critique of the New Age Movement, which offers alternative values and goals to the conventional cultural establishment. The author says this over-idealistic vision places too much emphasis on the personal, egotistical and conscious side, and does not acknowledge an imaginal or shadow side of life. Using archetypal psychology, which stresses metaphor, symbol and imagination, we are urged to look at taboos regarding sexuality and violence, thereby beginning to restore a more complete relationship with nature and life.

240pp   *43 illus.*   *paper*   £6.95   *(US $12.95)*

The Magic of Mind Power: *Awareness Techniques for the Creative Mind*   by Duncan McColl

This is a practical guide to the immense potential of the unconscious mind. It explains how and why visualisation, creative imagery and self-hypnosis work; areas now commonly used in the healing professions. This self-help guide tackles questions such as *Can I learn from my dreams? How do subliminal tapes work?*, and provides techniques which help to eliminate negative conditioning which can lead to bad health, lack of energy and low self-confidence.

192pp   *illus.*   *paper*   £4.95   *(US $10.95)*

Call No Man Master
by Joyce Collin-Smith

For more than 50 years, the author was closely involved with several well-known self-development groups, such as Moral Rearmament, Subud and Transcendental Meditation. Often with great humour, she shows how disillusioning and fallible can be these teachers and their followers, and that in the end one has to develop one's own inner teacher. A vivid recall of detail and personalities in the esoteric field of the '30s to the present.

240pp   *paper*   £6.95   *(US $13.95)*

A Rose to a Sick Friend: *A Positive Way to Approach Your Illness* by Tessa Goldhawk

This book offers a new way of coping with illness, pain, stress and worry. Written in a light style and interspersed with cartoons, jokes and exercises, it is nonetheless serious in purpose, the underlying message being that to some extent we create our own illnesses, and an understanding of this is the key to recovery. You are taken through a six-stage process, including accepting illness, learning from it, and learning to throw it off.

| 192pp | Illus. | paper | £5.95 | (US $10.95) |

Polarity Healing Handbook
by Wilfried Teschler

A good introduction to healing techniques, based on the principles of Polarity Therapy, of balancing the positive and negative energies of the body. It is set out to help you work with a partner, with explicit directions, exercises and details of treatments. It includes massage techniques and methods of working on the chakras, the energy centres of the body.

| 96pp | 93 photos | paper | £4.95 | (US $9.95) |

Journey through the Chakras: *Exercises for Healing and Internal Balancing* by Klausbernd Vollmar

This book holds the key to the body's energy balance, which is essential to health. A study of the energy centres, the chakras, is related to yoga and other disciplines or healing systems. There are self-help methods for working with energy, through yoga postures, visualisation techniques and meditation.

| 176pp | illus. | paper | £4.95 | (US $9.95) |

Reducing the Risk of Alzheimer's
by Michael Weiner PhD

An important background book on the degenerative disease that affects 1 in 8 of the population. Recent research has shown the connection between aluminum deposits in the brain and Alzheimer's, which is of great concern as aluminum is now a very common constituent in food preparation. The book includes a detailed program of preventative action for those in the early stages of the disease, and will give hope to many.

| 176pp | paper | £5.95 | (US $10.95) |

Please write us for a complete catalogue:
GATEWAY BOOKS, The Hollies, Wellow, Bath. BA2 8QJ
or in the USA:
The Great Tradition. 750 Adrian Way, San Rafael. CA 94903